# CARTOON ANIMATION:
# INTRODUCTION TO A CAREER

Milton Gray

Published by LION'S DEN PUBLICATIONS, INC.,
P.O. BOX 7368, Northridge, CA  91327-7368

Printed in the United States of America

Library of Congress Catalog Card Number 90-63934

Publisher's Cataloging in Publication
  (Prepared by Quality Books Inc.)

Gray, Milton, 1942-
    Cartoon animation: introduction to a career / Milton Gray. —
    p. cm.
    Includes bibliographical references and index.
    ISBN 0-9628444-5-4

    1. Animators— Vocational guidance.  2. Animated films. I.
Title.

NC1765                    741.58
              QBI90-142
              MARC

# CONTENTS

# TIME CHART

START
SCENE →

| | | | | |
|---|---|---|---|---|
| 1 | 24 | 44 | 66 | |
| 2 | | 45 | | |
| 3 | 25 | 46 | 67 | |
| 4 | 26 | 47 | 68 | |
| 5 | | 48 | | |
| 6 | 27 | 49 | 69 | |
| 7 | 28 | 50 | 70 | 84 |
| 8 | | 51 | 71 | 85 |
| 9 | 29 | 52 | 72 | 86 |
| 10 | 30 | 53 | 73 | 87 |
| 11 | 31 | 54 | 74 | 88 |
| 12 | 32 | 55 | 75 | 89 |
| 13 | 33 | 56 | 76 | 90 |
| 14 | 34 | 57 | 77 | 91 |
| 15 | 35 | 58 | 78 | 92 |
| 16 | 36 | 59 | 79 | 93 |
| 17 | 37 | 60 | 80 | 94 |
| 18 | 38 | 61 | 81 | 95 |
| 19 | 39 | 62 | 82 | 96 |
| 20 | 40 | 63 | 83 | 97 |
| 21 | 41 | 64 | | 98 |
| 22 | 42 | 65 | | 99 |
| 23 | 43 | | | 100 |
| | | | | 101 |
| | | | | 102 |
| | | | | 103 |
| | | | | 104 |
| | | | | 105 |
| | | | | 106 |
| | | | | 107 |

# FLIP BOOK

FLIP THESE DRAWINGS FROM BACK TO FRONT.

The action of this dog is fairly typical of Warner Bros. animation, as opposed to the more naturalistic Disney style. The dog is being threatened by a gang of tough cats. The drawings presented here are cleaned-up animation "extremes"; the intended timings of the missing "inbetween" drawings are indicated by "spacing charts" drawn alongside the extremes. (The timings of the swords and the gun are only approximated here, as they had to be fit in with the drawings of the dog in this book.)

Shown also is a strip of "exposure" instructions which would go to the camera-man. Each space down the strip represents one frame of movie film and every twenty-four frames represents one second of screen time. Some actions (as in drawings 1 through 10) are very fast and are shot on "ones" meaning that each drawing is shot for one frame only. Other actions (as in drawings 11 through 41) are slower and can be shot on "twos" — meaning each drawing is shot on two consecutive frames—and the action will still look smooth.

Some actions are especially fast, and are meant to be "felt" by the audience but not seen. Drawings 43 through 47 represent one example of a fluid "take", which is more elaborate (more varied) than the simple squash-into-anticipation and stretch-into-

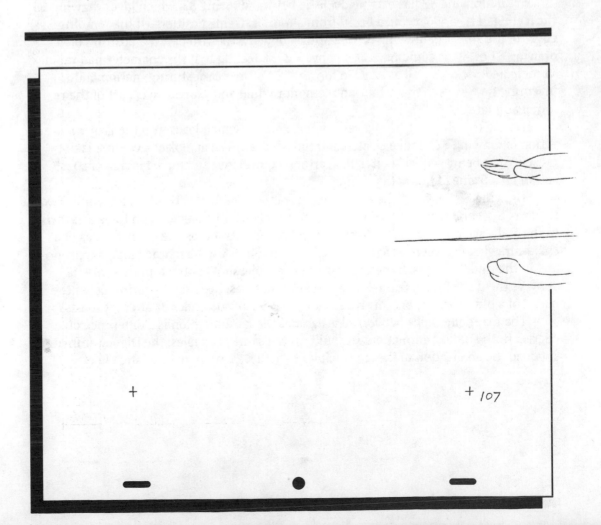

+

+ 107

surprise. Notice that in these stretched and squashed drawings, the volume of the head remains the same.

Drawings 86 through 90 represent an example of trembling fright within a slightly extended anticipation; in these drawings, as they are projected at twenty-four frames per second, the different head positions will flicker by too rapidly for any of them to be consciously seen, but the audience will feel the effect of a violent, stacatto tremble.

Even though, in drawings 43 through 47 and 86 through 90, none of the rapidly changing head positions will be consciously seen, there is an important difference in the fact that the shapes have been distorted in drawings 43 through 47, and not distorted in drawings 86 through 90. The distorted drawings will give a fluid feeling of an object in rapid motion, whereas the undistorted drawings will give a stacatto feeling of an object which has moved but jerked to a sudden stop between each movement. Only when several consecutive drawings are in some way similar, as in drawings 11 through 41, will undistored drawings appear to be in continuous fluid motion.

Drawings 82, 84 and 92 are examples of "smears": distorted drawings which give to very fast actions a greater feeling of fluidity than do undistorted drawings (which suddenly "pop" across a significant space), or even undistorted drawings which include "speed lines" trailing after them. These "smears", when used with a degree of inventiveness, can convey a sort of caricature of motion; for example, the "leading edge" of the "smear" in drawing 82 has extended a little beyond drawing 83, which gives drawing 83 the feeling of having "recoiled back" from a more extreme position. (If the "trailing edge" of the smear of drawing 82 had also extended backward past the position of drawing 81 or 80, it could have also conveyed the feeling that the character had rapidly "anticipated back" as well as "zipped forward".) For me, caricaturing motion and inventing new ways to make motion seem more fluid and expressive is part of the real fun of animation.

Notice that drawing 81 is a very slight "smear", which leads into the larger smear action of drawing 82; unlike stretch and squash drawings, an object's volume is not presented as being "equal"— it is the cartoon equivalent of a blurred image of a fast action on a frame of live-action film.

Drawing 83 has been "held" for fifteen frames, nearly two thirds of a second. Two thirds of a second may not sound like much time, but it is long enough to be a surprise to the audience for a character to suddenly "freeze". (As few as five or six frames of a "held" drawing will register a quick stop in an action.) A sudden dead stop, if appropriate, in the middle of fast, frenetic action can be a pleasing contrast. In this case, it conveys the dog's frozen fear (slowly realizing that, yes, he really is staring down the barrel of a blunderbuss) and his indecision whether to surrender or attempt to escape.

The main difference between Warner and Disney animation is a difference of degree. Both studios' animation was built on the same principles; the Disney animators subdued the application of those principles to achieve a more naturalistic effect.

# INTRODUCTION

(Continued from back cover.)

Animation theatrical production is presently booming in Hollywood, and the studios are searching for many more qualified artists. This current upsurge in production is fueled also by the growing home video market, which has become as profitable to Hollywood as the theatrical market. Theatrical cartoons released on home video are much more likely than live action to be purchased, rather than rented, on the expectation that children will want to watch them over and over. The hope is that more of the new cartoon films in production will be aimed at broader, more adult audiences.

Currently beginning production in Los Angeles are the following full animation theatrical features:

Walt Disney Pictures: *Beauty and the Beast* (plus a third Roger Rabbit short, *Hare in My Soup*). Several more theatrical features are in the development stage, including *Aladdin*, and a sequel to *Who Framed Roger Rabbit?*

Kroyer Films: *Fern Gully*—subtitled *The Last Rainforest*, this film has an ecological theme.

Hyperion Productions: *Rover Dangerfield*—this features a dog character based on the personality of Rodney Dangerfield.

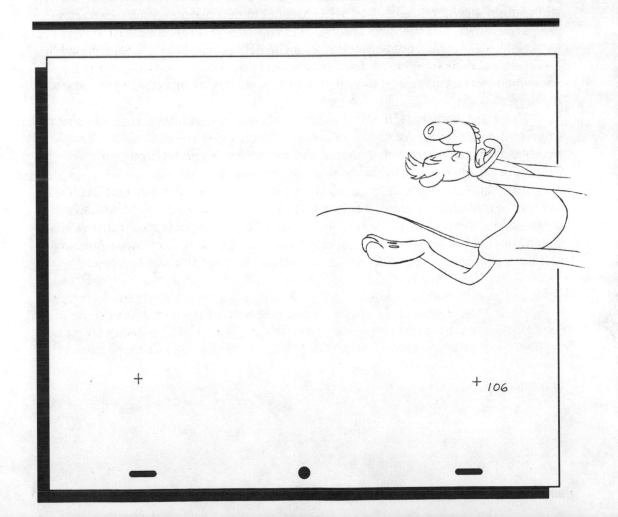

Hanna-Barbera Productions: *The Endangered*—this has an environmental theme.

Film Roman Inc.: *Tom and Jerry*—based on the 1940s M-G-M cartoon cat and mouse team.

In addition to these theatrical features, several Los Angeles studios are also increasing enormously the amount of television animation production, for adult prime time, including *The Simpsons* at Klasky-Csupo Productions and *Family Dog* at Amblin Entertainment, and for children on Saturday morning network and weekday syndication programs. Although the television shows are animated in foreign countries (primarily in the Pacific Rim), the shows are first written, storyboarded, and in many cases (including *The Simpsons* and *Family Dog*) completed in layout (full-production-size pencil drawings of backgrounds and characters for every scene in the film) before being sent overseas to be animated, all of which employs a very large number of artists in Los Angeles.

Beyond Los Angeles, other theatrical features are also being animated, and are employing several American animation artists, at studios including Amblin Productions in London, and Sullivan-Bluth Studios in Dublin, Ireland.

This book was written over a period of 20 years, combining different perspectives as I advanced as a professional in the Hollywood animation studios, from an inbetweener to a journeyman animator, to a director, animation writer and producer. As a beginner, struggling alongside other beginners, I came to know intimately the full range of difficulties a beginner faces, and slowly discovered solutions to problems that still confront beginners today. It is difficult, if not impossible, for a veteran who has long since overcome a beginner's problems to reconstruct them accurately and write with real insight about specific solutions. Fortunately I chose to write about these problems and their solutions in detail back when I was still encountering them. In subsequent years, I continued to augment and update this information, all the way to my present position as director/producer.

I have purposely kept this book as brief and direct as possible, so that the most important points would not be lost in verbiage. I have a very complete collection of books and magazines on animation, and can say without hesitation that over 90 percent of the information in this book is not available anywhere else.

An additional feature of this book is the "flip book" which demonstrates some of the special movement of cartoon animation. While some Disney books include examples of animation that are quite close to literal live-action photography, the animation in this book incorporates several principles more typical of the Warner Bros. style, and is accompanied by a detailed explanation (beginning on page one).

# ABOUT THE AUTHOR:

Milton Gray is a professional animator, director, writer and producer, who has worked on 16 theatrical features, from Walt Disney's *The Jungle Book* (1967) to Steven Spielberg's *Poltergeist* (1982) at Lucasfilm, and has directed numerous television shows, from *Thundar* (1981) to *The Simpsons* (1990).

From 1969 to 1980 Mr. Gray worked closely with researcher/writer Michael Barrier on collecting and preserving the knowledge of animation production as it was practiced during the mid-1930s through the mid-1950s—the Golden Age of animation. Together Mr. Gray and Mr. Barrier interviewed on tape over 200 of the most prominent and innovative animators, directors, writers, producers, designers and technicians from that era, virtually all of whom are currently retired or deceased.

In 1985 Mr. Gray joined in partnership with animator/producer Al Lowenheim to create and produce cartoon films which would equal and surpass the achievements of animation's Golden Age, at their studio, Lion's Den.

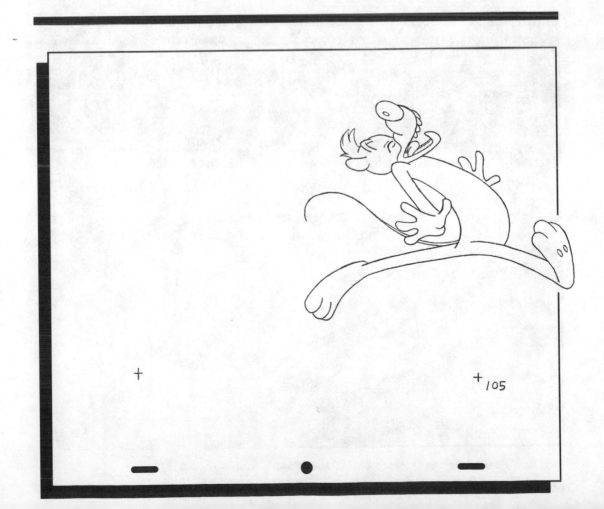

105

# ACKNOWLEDGMENTS

In 1966, when I was still an inbetweener at the Disney Studio, I began corresponding with Mike Barrier, the publisher and, at that time, the sole writer of *Funnyworld,* the first scholarly magazine on animation. Mike's careful observation of human nature and art added enormously to my critical thinking, and our ongoing correspondence caused me to analyze and write down everything I learned about animation, as I was learning it. Some years later, Mike urged me to compile my notes into a book, and helped to structure the first draft. Over several more years, as I continued to add new material, Mike has patiently offered suggestions at each new stage.

The final version has also benefited from the suggestions of several more people, each of them highly knowledgeable in their respective fields: my partner (at Lion's Den Productions) Al Lowenheim, artist and writer Paul Gruwell, cartoon director Eddie Fitzgerald, comics publisher Steve Schanes, Business Representative of the Motion Picture Screen Cartoonists Union (Los Angeles) Steve Hulett, and the man whose own animation book—and later, books—were my guiding light since early childhood, Preston Blair.

Frank Mutascio, of Mutascio Graphics in San Diego, designed this book, and Janet Cummings did the color styling for the front cover.

*Bugs Bunny in Bob Clampett's* **What's Cookin' Doc?** *(1944)*    ©Warner Bros. Cartoons, Inc.

This book was also influenced to varying degrees by a great many other people who shared their knowledge with me, throughout my career in the animation industry. I would particularly like to mention the animators who personally taught me and many others, in their homes and after hours: Benny Washam, Art Babbitt, Irv Spence and Cliff Nordberg.

And I would especially like to express my deep gratitude to the late Bob Clampett, a genuinely inspired director of many of the great Warner Bros. cartoons of the 1930s and 1940s, for his personal friendship and the generosity of his time and knowledge for so many years.

In this increasingly litigious age, authors and publishers are advised to post disclaimers to protect themselves from frivolous lawsuits. Here, then, is our official...

# WARNING—DISCLAIMER

This book cannot and does not represent to guarantee employment in the animation industry. Such employment is dependent upon a number of factors, including the amount of new work needed to be done beyond what the already employed personnel can handle, the basic abilities of the applicant, and the applicant's willingness to cooperate in a team effort.

This book is designed to provide information in regard to the subject matter covered. It is sold with the understanding that the publisher and author are not engaged in rendering legal, accounting or other professional services. If legal or other expert assistance is required, the services of a competent professional should be sought.

It is not the purpose of this manual to reprint all the information that is otherwise available to the author and/or publisher, but to complement, amplify and supplement other texts. You are urged to read all the available material, learn as much as possible about cartoon filmmaking and to tailor the information to your individual needs. For more information, see the many references in the Bibliography.

Every effort has been made to make this manual as complete and as accurate as possible. However, there *may be mistakes* both typographical and in content. Therefore, this text should be used only as a general guide and not as the ultimate source of animation/ cartoon filmmaking information. Furthermore, this manual contains information on animation/cartoon filmmaking only up to the printing date.

The purpose of this manual is to educate and entertain. The author and Lion's Den Publications shall have neither liability nor responsibility to any person or entity with respect to any loss or damage caused, or alleged to be caused, directly or indirectly by the information contained in this book.

*If you do not wish to be bound by the above, you may return this book to the publisher for a full refund.*

# PART ONE:
# GETTING INTO THE BUSINESS

# I. EMPLOYMENT OPPORTUNITIES FOR THE BEGINNER

Most people who aspire to a lifetime career in animation are motivated by the joy they experienced from having seen some of the best theatrical cartoons from the late 1930s, the 1940s and the early 1950s (even if they initially saw them as re-releases on television). People's tastes vary, and for some the favorite cartoons are the best of the Fleischers or U.P.A. or M-G-M. For others, like myself, the favorite cartoons are the best of Disney and Warners.

But the industry changes continually, for reasons that will be explained in these pages. The relative ease or difficulty of marketing cartoon films certainly affects the degree of success of the industry, but the larger factors controlling success are the abilities and initiatives of the creative people, particularly the animators, directors and writers.

Employment in animation is presently booming in Los Angeles. New people are being absorbed into the industry at a record rate, and the present high level of employment is likely to continue for at least several more years.

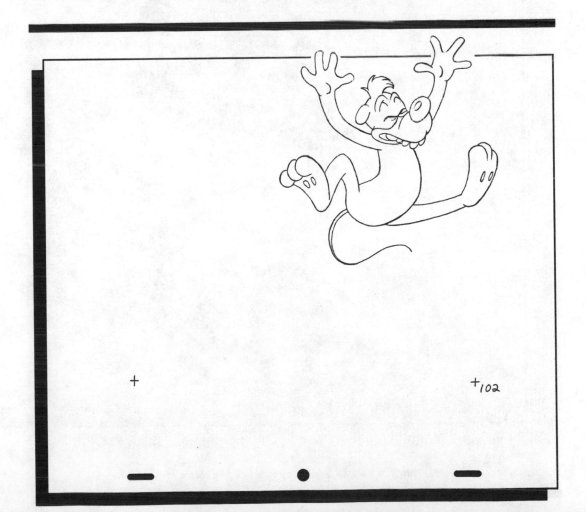

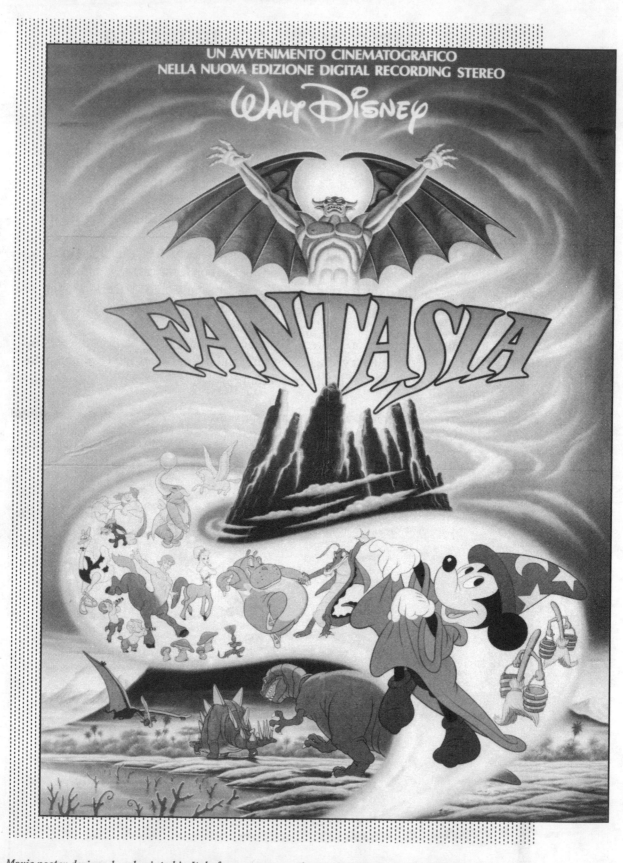

*Movie poster designed and printed in Italy for a recent re-release of* **Fantasia**. ©Walt Disney Productions

This is somewhat surprising to those of us who have worked in the industry during the past decade; throughout most of the 1980s, the employment picture looked increasingly bleak, while the product got increasingly worse. Indeed, the economics of the animation industry have fluctuated wildly over the past decades, and a great many talented people who were initially attracted to animation have left in despair.

The entire motion picture industry is undergoing dramatic marketing and economic changes. To what degree will these changes affect the future production of high quality animation? How did the animation industry's circumstances get so bad before, and how can we be reasonably certain that things will not fall apart again? I think the best way to answer these questions is to begin with a brief historical overview.

Cartoon animation began as a crude novelty, and achieved moderate success, in fits and starts, only in direct proportion to the quality of the story ideas and artistic expression of its best practitioners—and in competition with the best that live-action film had to offer, especially since animation and live action tended to be shown on the same programs, in the same theaters.

The major breakthrough occurred during the mid-to-late 1930s, as the lack of other jobs during the Great Depression forced many of the nation's best artists into the animation business, primarily at the Walt Disney Studio, which actively sought out better artists through a nationwide recruiting program. The late 1930s and early 1940s, at Disney's and some of the other studios, were certainly the Golden Age of animation, the era when most of the greatest minds that have ever been attracted to this art form

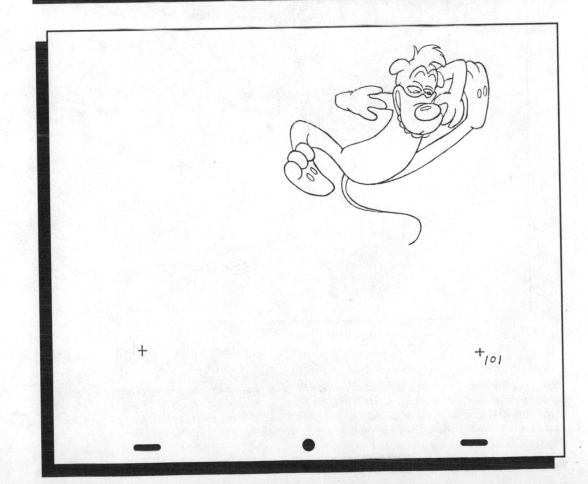

*Model sheet for Private Snafu, a character featured in several full-animation cartoons made by the Schlesinger/Warner studio during World War II for the U.S. Military. Like the Warner theatrical cartoons of the mid-1940's, some of the Snafu cartoons are terrific—and Snafu is continually facing the problems that confront military men. These cartoons have just recently become available in home video (see Bibliography).*

worked closely together, experimenting and building on each other's discoveries. The sheer artistry and production values generated a tremendous excitement among the public and the industry alike; the writing also improved significantly, but unfortunately not as much as the visual artistry, and so after a few years the enthusiasm for cartoon films began to wane, especially as the writing in live action features continued to improve and, at its best, surpassed that of the cartoons. The lack of better writing (or writing more suitable to older audiences) in Disney's feature length cartoons is especially tragic (more on this in chapters four and five), and many of the artists became increasingly disillusioned working for the dictatorial Walt. Sadly, no other animation producers took up the opportunity to improve the writing of their films significantly beyond the best of Disney. During World War II many of the best artists in animation were drafted, largely into the production of military training films; the postwar economy allowed most of them to move into artistic fields outside of animation, and the animation industry simply coasted on its past achievements, repeating old formulas (of writing and drawing) until marketing changes broke its momentum completely.

A surprising number of young people today who see the old theatrical shorts re-released on television—and the best of the classic Disney feature length cartoons re-released in the theaters—are unaware that those cartoons were in fact produced so many decades ago. Cases in point: Disney's *Snow White and the Seven Dwarfs, Pinocchio, Fantasia, Dumbo,* and *Bambi* were all released between 1937 and 1942, and Disney's *Cinderella, Alice in Wonderland, Peter Pan, Lady and the Tramp,* and *Sleep-*

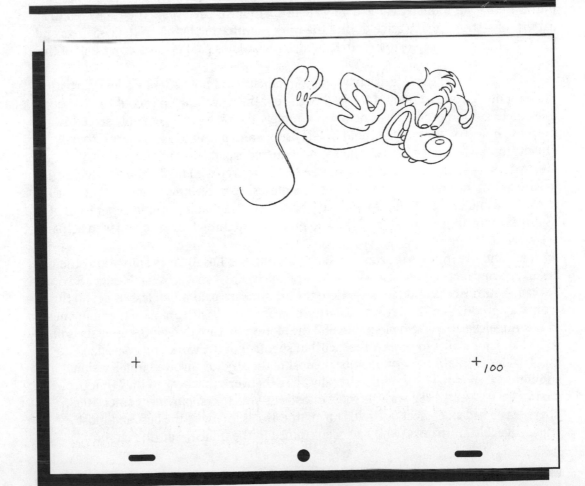

*ing Beauty* were released between 1950 and 1959; and most of the theatrical shorts (Disney's, Warner's, M-G-M's and others') were produced between 1930 and 1960.

The marketing change that contributed most significantly to the demise of the theatrical short cartoons resulted from a legal action taken by the federal government in 1948, which dictated that theatrical movie studios could no longer own their own theaters, which in turn meant that films had to be rented individually to the theaters rather than marketed as a package of a feature and a few short subjects. Theater managers increasingly took the position that only feature length films attracted audiences, and eventually discontinued renting shorts. At the Disney studio, the drop in quality of the cartoon features after *Sleeping Beauty* was the result of Walt Disney's personal lack of interest and involvement in cartoon film production in the last years before his death in 1966.

In 1963, the American animation industry suffered its worst year for unemployment. There was relatively little animation being done for television then, but by 1967 TV animation had started to boom in Los Angeles, and the growth continued into about the mid 1970s. For the first time since the early 1950s, new people were brought into the industry in sizable numbers. Unfortunately, most of the work in the 1970s was commissioned by the three major commercial television networks at very low budgets and, in contrast to the year-round release schedule of the earlier theatrical market, the commercial networks ran most of their new shows only during certain months each year (beginning in September). The networks would not commission the following year's programs until around April of that year, and, consequently, most of the people in the animation industry worked only about six months each year. They adjusted to a pattern of setting money aside during the work months and living on their savings and California State unemployment funds (which the studios paid for) the other half of the year.

The growth of the television animation industry did not generate a lot of artistic excitement. Anyone who loved the best of the old theatrical cartoons could easily see that the television product was not even remotely the same, and generally stayed away from the industry. Worse, the trend in television animation then was toward the illustration-style "super heros," and so the industry expanded primarily with failed illustrators—people who could not succeed in their preferred fields, and whose attitude toward animation ranged from complete disinterest to sneering contempt. Worse still, toward the end of the 1970s, the industry began to attract an emerging generation of "Saturday morning TV retards": kids who grew up watching that stuff and who actually preferred it.

Around the mid 1970s, starting slowly at first, the Los Angeles animation studios began subcontracting television work to foreign studios—in Australia, Mexico, Spain, Taiwan, South Korea and Japan—where the artists were paid much less. By 1980 this "runaway production" had reached alarming proportions, with animation employment in Los Angeles declining rapidly. In 1982 the Motion Picture Screen Cartoonists union staged a major strike to protest the fact that so much of the work was unavailable to Los Angeles animation union members. Most of the studios involved in television animation responded by sending virtually all of the work that year to the foreign studios. As a result, 1982 was the most disastrous year for employment since 1963. There was a bad side effect, as well. During the 1970s, many of the best and most knowledgeable animators, who had been trained in the industry during its most important growth period in the 1930s, had begun retiring. In 1982, rather than face walking in the Los Angeles summer heat for weeks in picket lines, nearly all of the rest of the best animators from the 1930s retired. Although some of the younger animators are also talented, few of them have received any real animation training, and of those few, most have had to get it entirely on their own, outside the studios, sometimes taking private lessons in the homes of the few older animators willing to teach. Thus, 1982 truly marked the end of an era.

In 1984 the employment picture improved temporarily, thanks to the growth of a new marketplace for original television programing: syndication to the mushrooming numbers of new independent television stations in the United States, which could compete rather effectively with the original three television networks in terms of collective revenues (and which—so far—do not adhere as rigidly to programing "seasons" as the three networks). Since then, however, the number of available foreign studios increased, and so the employment picture in Los Angeles became as depressed as before. Added to that, mainland China, with one quarter of the world's population, is opening its doors to trade with the United States, including the subcontracting of television animation from American studios, and the pay of animation artists in China is far lower even than the pay of artists in other foreign countries.

Since 1960, over thirty non-Disney theatrical feature length cartoons have been made in California—two of them in the San Francisco area, the rest in Los Angeles—but the pattern has been that most of them were made by studios that came into being

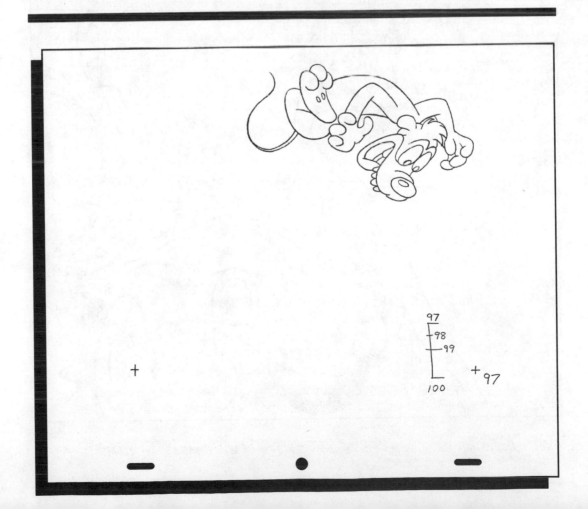

just for the production of a single feature film and then closed down. Worse, all of these films were produced and directed by people who either were not interested in creating a quality product or were interested in quality but lacked the knowledge and understanding necessary to make a good film. This has resulted in films that, almost without exception, have been artistic and financial failures—which made it increasingly difficult to attract investment financing to produce more cartoon features—which had a disasterous effect on animation employment. (Chapters four through six address the fundamentals of better cartoon filmmaking.)

The great resurgence of production of theatrical full animation in Los Angeles occurred immediately following the enormous commercial success of Disney's *Who Framed Roger Rabbit?* in the summer of 1988. The Disney Studio alone is now turning out one large-budget cartoon theatrical feature per year, plus an occasional theatrical short and featurette, and at least four other cartoon studios in Los Angeles are now in production on one theatrical feature each.

Why isn't the theatrical feature animation presently being subcontracted to foreign countries to save money, as is the case with American television animation, especially as the animators in foreign countries continue to improve their skills? American animators have one potential edge over their foreign counterparts—although the potential is important only to the degree that the writing for animation

*Detail of Jessica from the nation-wide newspaper ads in 1988 for* **Who Framed Roger Rabbit?**
©*Touchstone Pictures and Amblin Entertainment, Inc.*

films is respectable enough to utilize it: Audiences are typically most interested in themselves and in their own culture, and the United States represents 50 to 60 percent of the total worldwide boxoffice revenue. American animators, being intimately familiar with American culture, can best capture in cartoon caricature the important nuances of body language and facial expressions, especially in English-speaking dialog acting scenes.

How long will the current resurgence of theatrical animation production in Los Angeles continue? Given its present momentum, plus the determination of the current management of the Disney Studio, it will probably last for several more years, but whether it will continue to the end of the present decade is dubious, in my opinion, if the writing and animation do not improve significantly. Animation is succeeding commercially today as a novelty with the post baby-boomer theatrical audience, especially following the absence of any significant new theatrical cartoons in the previous twenty years; but, as happened in the 1940s, the audience will eventually tire of the novelty if the writing, in particular, does not improve to the level of the best in live action films.

For example, *Who Framed Roger Rabbit?* was sadly deficient in the areas of writing, direction and animation, in ways that overlapped and undermined each other. The central character, Roger, apart from being abrasive, had no real personality; substituted for personality was only a shallow gimmick of a sputtering voice. Jessica was obviously intended to be an erotic character, but she was so poorly designed as to

be simply ugly and grotesque—and not in the least erotic. (The drawings of her in the newspaper ads in 1988 were far better than any of the drawings of her in the film.) The plot's climax was essentially nothing more imaginative than the two lead characters waiting to be sprayed by a hose. Most of the animation was lacking in the sense that the various characters' "acting" was not convincing. (By contrast, in the old 1940s and 1950s Warner cartoons, even the crazy Daffy Duck, no matter how manic he became, still seemed fully motivated and "sincere" in nearly everything he did.) Much of the animation direction was unclear in the sense that in most cases the fast actions did not "read"; even I, as an experienced animator in the audience, had difficulty following many of the actions. (By contrast, the directors and animators of the old 1940s and 1950s Warner cartoons had learned, through experimentation in the late 1930s, how to "stage" even lightning-fast actions so that they would read clearly. The people working on *Roger Rabbit* had available to them all the achievements recorded in those earlier films, yet they did not incorporate any of them in most of their scenes.)

I might also mention, although this is arguably more a matter of personal taste than objective criticism, that the tone of the entire *Roger Rabbit* feature was extremely mean-spirited—which is emphatically *not* in keeping with the vast majority of the cartoons of the 1940s, which the film was trying to emulate. I mention this because it seemed to me that the mean-spiritedness was used as a cheap substitute in the absence

*The Simpsons*. Intelligent adult writing and thoughtful direction have made this an extremely successful prime-time cartoon TV series.   ©20th Century-Fox Film Corp.

of honest wit.

So why was the *Roger Rabbit* feature such an enormous commercial success if the film was so poorly written, directed and animated? I believe the film succeeded commercially by default, in the absence of any other decent product of its kind. Plus the film was a novelty, being the most elaborate combination of animation and live action in history (at the unprecedented cost of over $50,000,000) . Plus the film was very heavily advertised and promoted, and prominently displayed the names of both the Disney Studio and Steven Spielberg.

Disney's next major commercial success in animation, *The Little Mermaid* (1989), was significantly better in writing and animation, but at best the writing was still trite. Unfortunately, the writing in the theatrical cartoons of Disney's closest competitor, the Sullivan-Bluth Studio, has been considerably worse. The only on-going good writing for animation in immediate history has been for the prime time television series, *The Simpsons* (which began Christmas week, 1989). The writing for *The Simpsons* has been so good that the show has become the most successful of any category—cartoon or live action—on the Fox TV Network and has been a popular topic of conversation both inside and outside the animation industry. As good an example as it is, though, the show itself is being produced on the same low budget as a Saturday morning TV series, which allows no elaboration in the animation—which, in turn, largely confines the writing to verbal humor.

Cost of production is always an important factor in any proposal for a cartoon

project. A future economic aid to the industry will be "electronic coloring" by computers that scan pencil line drawings and fill in each individual area with any color desired. These computer-colored drawings can then be combined with each other and with rendered backgrounds as a single composite picture. The composite can be shown in video or transferred to motion picture film for theatrical release. The cost of electronic coloring is presently higher than the traditional method of tracing or photocopying animation drawings onto clear sheets of acetate, called "cels," and painting the necessary colors onto those cels. Cel painting is tedious work, and because it is so time-consuming it represents about one third of the total cost of producing a cartoon film in the United States. But the expectation is that computer technology, which has already been used to good visual effect in portions of live-action and cartoon films, will soon evolve into a cost-efficient method of coloring animation. In fact, the Disney Studio is already pursuing this technology for regular use; their most recent theatrical cartoon feature, *The Rescuers Down Under,* released November 1990, was colored entirely on computer.

An expanding marketplace effectively offsets the risk of financial investment, which makes financing for new product less difficult to obtain. The arrival of the video industry—prerecorded videotape cassettes and laser videodiscs—has extended the market for theatrical product to the older, "stay-at-home" audience, which has already

*Brad Bird's **The Family Dog,** telecast in 1987 as a single half-hour cartoon segment in Steven Spielberg's weekly TV series, **Amazing Stories**. The cartoon was a rarity in the 1980s, combining good writing and skillful direction with very competent animation.* ©Amblin TV Inc. and Universal City Studio, Inc.

become as profitable to Hollywood as the theater audience, and is continuing to grow.

One might hope that the video industry would eventually make possible the production financing and distribution of new shorts—or perhaps collections of shorts, in a sort of monthly "video magazine" format. Artistically, the thought is especially tantalizing as one also anticipates the arrival of high definition video tape and laser disc players, plus high definition monitors (TV sets with a picture quality greatly superior to present television); these are expected to enter the U S. consumer market within the next few years, even though high definition television broadcasting may still be a decade away.

If animation employment is likely, for the above reasons, to continue to be available to skilled, qualified artists, how does a beginner begin?

Animation training (especially good animation training) is very difficult to find, since animation is such a specialized field. But good draftsmanship—being able to draw many things well—is the basis for practically everything in the business. (Much more will be said about that in chapters two and three.) In the Golden Age, animation salaries were so small that employers could afford to train on the job. But today, union-controlled salaries are so high that on-the-job training is almost unthinkable. (I'm not anti union—I feel that salaries need to be high to compete with other fields to attract the best talent.) Presently the Motion Picture Screen Cartoonists union in Los Angeles is conducting classes on a regular basis, in every category of cartoon film production;

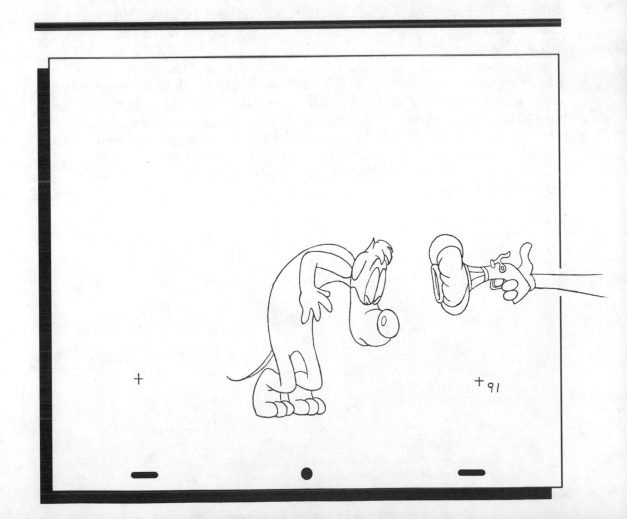

these classes are available for a nominal fee to people outside the industry who want to work in a studio, although priority for admission is given to union members who want to improve their skills.

This book has been written about animation, and the training and problems that are unique to animation, but it might be well to mention here that there are three other smaller categories of art jobs in the animation studios that require a less specialized, more traditional kind of art school education. One is called "layout," which involves making full production-size pencil drawings of the backgrounds for every scene in the film, plus one or two drawings of the characters in the proper costumes, and in the proper size and perspective to fit the backgrounds, to guide the animators. Another category is called "background," which involves making full color paintings (usually in acrylics or opaque watercolor) to match the layout artists' pencil drawings of the settings. The third category is called "storyboard," which requires drawing the cartoon story (usually from a written script) much like a comic strip. In animation studios with low budgets and tight schedules, the storyboards may be followed closely throughout production, with few changes being made, so the storyboard artist needs to be very familiar with film direction.

Animation studios exist in a large number of cities across the United States, and in most cases are involved in making cartoon television commercials and animated industrial films for local business and industry. The focus of this book is on the large-budget Hollywood entertainment cartoons. However, there is an annually updated *Animation Industry Directory,* which lists studios and services nationwide; for more information, write: Expanded Entertainment, P.O. Box 25547, Los Angeles, California 90025.

To locate studios in Los Angeles, the easiest way is to contact the Motion Picture Screen Cartoonists union, at 4729 Lankershim Boulevard, North Hollywood, California 91602 for a current list of studios, because so many studios come into being for a short time and then go out of business. Even most of the ongoing studios have changed addresses surprisingly often. If the cartoonists union itself changes its address, the studios can still be found listed in the Los Angeles telephone directory, mostly in the volume titled "Northwest Area," and the Los Angeles phone books are available in public libraries in virtually every city in America.

better he or she will be able to translate such types and expressions convincingly into cartoon figures.

The art of cartooning is based in part on abstract design, an elegant and subtle combination of geometric shapes. Those shapes are arranged to suggest a caricature of a human, or an animal or an inanimate object, without losing the elegance of the basic abstract shapes. Then those shapes are distorted, not only stretched and squashed, but bent and twisted, to suggest, both broadly and subtly, different expressions, body gestures and attitudes. Animation (motion) can add a feeling of magic, as obviously two-dimensional drawings of three-dimensional shapes turn and revolve in seemingly three-dimensional space—and different parts of these complex three-dimensional shapes distort at slightly different times, and to varying degrees, suggesting ever changing reactions of the "character" to its environment.

To make the moving two-dimensional drawings look especially three-dimensional, the trick is not so much in adding shading but rather in continually moving the character or object "on all three axes." That is, think of the three dimensions of a cube—of its height, width and depth. Then think of those three dimensions as the three primary axes of a sphere—and keep the sphere moving not on just one axis—such as turning simply from left to right—but tilting while it turns, so that for example as a character's head turns from left to right we see first the crown of the head and then under the chin. Then add stretch and squash to the head for expression in dialog while turning the head "on all three axes," and do essentially the same with all parts of

the character's body. By doing this you will discover the beauty and magic of cartooning—and discover initially how difficult drawing a "simple" cartoon character can be.

It is useful to know that animation studios hire artists not on the basis of whether they graduated from a formal art school, but on the quality of their portfolios. The one thing that all animation studios look for in a new applicant's portfolio is pencil line drawings of the human figure. Do not copy cartoon characters from pictures in books for your portfolio, but do include some cartoon characters in *original poses,* acting out a short scene, as if in a comic strip. An interviewer, who is usually a professional cartoonist himself, can spot at a glance, in a sketch in pencil, whether the applicant was able to draw well quickly or if he had to labor over the drawing for a long time. And since all cartoon characters are based directly or indirectly on human anatomy, that becomes the common denominator—the single most important subject that a newcomer must be able to draw.

Attending art school is the most frequently recommended way to learn to draw. In an ideal situation, a very knowledgeable instructor will not only teach and inspire, but also help each student overcome individual "blind spots": the tendency to repeat the same mistakes. Further advantages, ideally, are the enrichment of new ideas, not only from the instructors but from the other students, and networking (outside the professional studios) with fellow artists and potential future business contacts.

Unfortunately, as in any field, not all instructors are ideal, and art is an especially

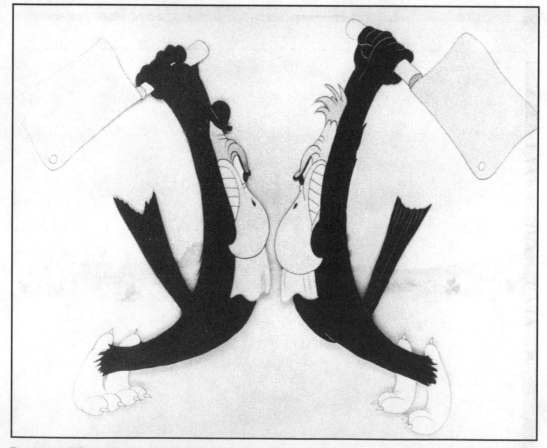

*Tex Avery's* **What's Buzzin' Buzzard** *(1943). Notice the simplicity yet elegance of the shapes in the design of these manic characters.* ©Loew's Incorporated

difficult subject, being not an exact science but entirely subjective, ethereal, and therefore it is difficult to formalize "rules" of art and drawing without stifling originality and creativity. This is true not only of "creative art" classes, but also of life drawing (human figure) classes, which one might expect to be so fundamental as to be much less open to opinion and interpretation (more on this a little later in this chapter). Some instructors have very limited abilities, and tend to be dogmatic or provide no instruction at all. If instruction in your life drawing class is minimal, you will probably find it very helpful to refer to the information in some of the how-to-draw books.

The how-to-draw books should be taken as lists of things to be aware of. They point out proportions, show how parts of the body fit together, and demonstrate the examples of form and the flow of gestures. In no case are they to be slavishly copied with the intention of making exact reproductions of the illustrations. Rather, the copying should be done with the intention of acquiring a comprehension—and committing to memory—the thousands of details of average anatomical shapes and proportions. It is much like memorizing the alphabet, or memorizing the musical scales; the purpose is to acquire a working knowledge of averages to measure against later when a drawing in class or in the studio starts to look "wrong." A few highly recommended books on drawing (with current prices as of 1990) are:

*Drawing the Head and Figure* by Jack Hamm, 1963, Putnam Publishing, $7.95 (paperback), *Figure Drawing For All It's Worth* by Andrew Loomis, 1943, Viking Press, $18.95, and *Drawing the Head and Hands* by Andrew Loomis, 1956, Viking Press,

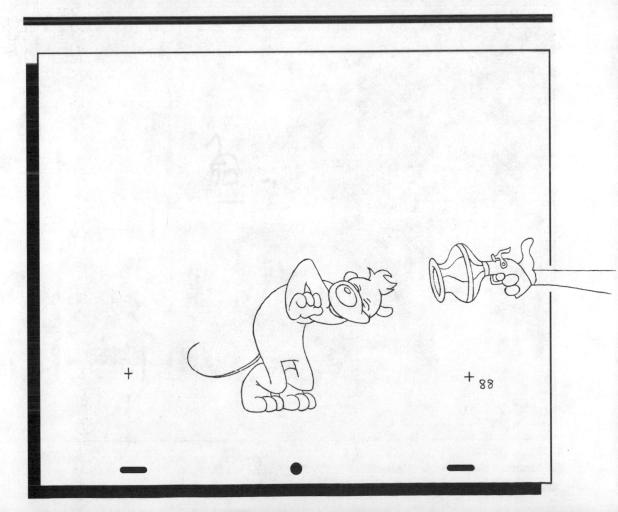

$18.95 are excellent books for demonstrating proportions of the human figure. (The two Andrew Loomis books have just recently gone out of print, for the first time in decades; hopefully they might be reprinted again.)

*Anatomy* by Joseph Sheppard, 1975, Watson-Guptill, $24.50, and *Artistic Anatomy* by Dr. Paul Richer and Robert Beverly Hale, 1971, Watson-Guptill, $22.50 (paperback) are excellent books on human anatomy, with detailed drawings; among other things, they show each major section of the body turned in several different directions.

*Drawing the Human Form* by William A. Berry, 1977, Prentice Hall Press, $19.95 (paperback) presents several different approaches to drawing, and to understanding the human form three-dimensionally, with particularly excellent drawings from a wide variety of sources.

*The Natural Way to Draw* by Kimon Nicolaides, 1941, Houghton Mifflin, $10.00 (paperback) combines a discussion of the art of drawing with a series of suggested exercises; it is intended to be used by students who are drawing from live models on a regular periodic basis.

*The Human Figure—A Photographic Reference for Artists* by Erik A. Ruby, 1974, Van Nostrand Reinhold, $24.95 (paperback) is a collection of over six hundred photographs of nude models in poses that are particularly useful to artists for study and reference.

*How to Draw Animals* by Jack Hamm, 1969, Putnam Publishing, $7.95 (paper-

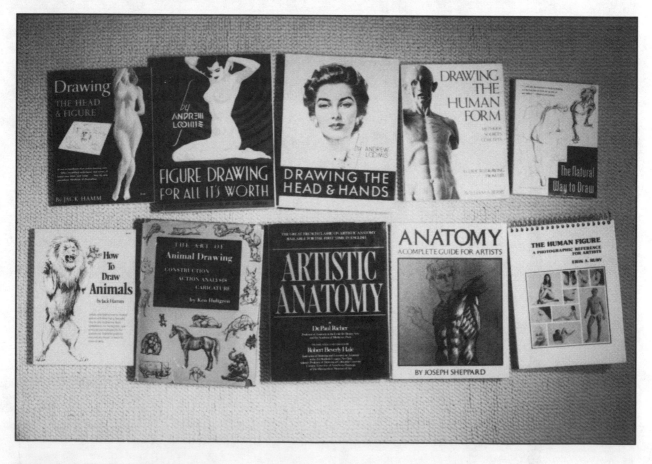

*Recommended books on how to draw.*

back) and *The Art of Animal Drawing* by Ken Hultgren, 1950, McGraw-Hill (currently out of print, but available in some libraries), are particularly useful to aspiring animators because they include descriptions and drawings of various animal actions including walks and runs. Ken Hultgren, in fact, was an animator on Disney's *Bambi*.

Some art school students who practice drawing exclusively from models become very adept at "copying from life," but are lost when asked to make a drawing without a model. Most animation work requires making many drawings a day without the aid of models, although animators and their assistants are provided with "model sheets" which show each cartoon character from a few different angles.

The earliest months in learning to draw can be the most discouraging. The beginner is usually unaware of the degree of the complexities and subtleties in the shapes of the human figure. In the opening chapter of *The Natural Way to Draw*, Kimon Nicolaides states, "The sooner you make your first five thousand mistakes, the sooner you will be able to correct them." In *Drawing the Head and Figure* (page 39) Jack Hamm states, "After considerable practice you will be able to sense the proportions."

You will find that after learning the basics of drawing the figure, your powers of observation will increase to the point that you will learn by watching people even when you are not drawing. Several cartoonists recommend building a reference sketchbook of character "types" by sitting along a busy sidewalk and sketching the different kinds of people who walk by—their faces, their postures, their "costumes." This practice goes

an important step beyond learning the basics of formula character drawing, and beyond the drawing of a few basic facial expressions (which I call "the six-mask school of cartooning").

Capturing the *transition* between one expression (emotion) and another—for example, a character who was fearful but is just *beginning* to realize a possible solution—this is a subtlety of acting (in drawing) that conveys to the audience that the character has a mind, a complex thought process, a specific personality. This is part of what I call the (emotional) *tone* of a drawing. As discussed elsewhere in this book, good writing—and specifically the tone of the writing—is to the public the single most important part of a cartoon film, but the audience never sees the script—only the drawings, which must capture and communicate the tone of the script. In a good cartoon drawing, the exact way a character stands, his body language, his expression, and the condition of his clothes tell us *everything* about that individual: his past, what he's lived through, and what kind of person he is today.

As a practical matter, you will find it advantageous to commit to memory how to draw a great many different types of humans, costumes, animals, props and settings, because a professional cartoonist is frequently asked to sketch a great many different things in a hurry, without time to hunt for reference material. To test your ability, select a news story out of a newspaper and try to draw it as a comic strip. Can you draw the characters, their actions, their costumes, the props, the locations?

Hypothetical question: If someone gave you just enough money to adequately produce the cartoon of your dreams, whom would you hire? Would you hire you (or an exact duplicate of yourself), or would you prefer to hire a better draftsman? That's the question an employer asks himself about you when you apply for a job.

I HATE TO DRAW the realistic human figure.

Most people who draw the illustration style human figure do so because they love to. To them every nuance of shape of the elbows, wrists and ankles is a source of fascination. Some people have stated that they get euphorically high from exploring the infinite nuances of the human form with pencil and with modeling clay.

But most of the people who love to draw the realistic human figure disdain cartoon drawing, partly because cartoons "are not real." The opposite is also true: Many people who love to draw cartoons tend to dislike drawing realistic human figures because "that is not creating anything new—why copy something that already exists?"

People who disdain cartoons are very unlikely to become the best cartoonists. As in any field of art, the best work is invariably done by those who deeply love what they're doing. However, the best cartoons are drawn by people who have enough knowledge of real human and animal figures to be able to draw them well. This is because good cartooning is rooted in reality, right down to the most elusive gestures and expressions.

This creates an enormous problem for a lot of potential cartoonists: the emotional conflict of having to learn to do well something that one actually dislikes, but which is almost impossible to learn unless one does genuinely like it. I have been one of those people, so perhaps I can offer insights from my own experience.

It is interesting, and perhaps significant, to note that the physical proportions of some of the Disney and nearly all of the Warner cartoon characters correspond directly to the proportionate sensitivities of the human nervous system (see page 75 of the book, *Drawing the Human Form,* listed above), and probably for that reason their proportions feel very correct: their heads are disproportionately large relative to their bodies, and their eyes and mouths are disproportionately large on their heads, especially in the case of Bugs Bunny and Donald Duck. (These same proportions also correspond to that in most primitive art.) In my own experience, when I finally faced having to draw realistic humans (after drawing cartoons only, for several years), I had a particularly difficult time adjusting to realistic human proportions. For one thing, I kept instinctively trying to draw people's eyes too big and near the tops of their heads, instead of at the center of their heads. In drawings, the realistic human head seemed unfamiliarly and annoyingly small, being only one eighth the height of the total figure, and the eyes especially tiny on the head, to the extent of not even being decent-sized dots, but barely more than tiny specks of pencil graphite. It took a heck of a lot of practice and frustration for me to learn to draw those tiny eyes, with accuracy and expression, on those giant bodies.

The individual who decides, at the age of twenty or later, to begin to learn to draw the realistic human figure (especially if he or she doesn't like to draw it) will likely face another severe problem: the absolute lack of moral support from family and friends. Everybody who learns to draw makes the same beginner mistakes; it is unavoidable. But to the beginner at age six, everybody says, "Oh look, he's drawing so *well* for a six-year-old!" At age twenty, a beginner making the same beginner mistakes is told, "That's awful—you shouldn't be drawing, you obviously have no talent for that!"

The beginner at age twenty attending life drawing class is likely to encounter a few other people about the same age who have been drawing on their own since age six. But these people say, "Oh, I've never taken a drawing class before in my life," implying, "I've never picked up a pencil before today." And they say, "Drawing just comes naturally to me," which implies, "I have that magic quality called talent. You obviously do not." Some of these people become art teachers, and then their pronouncements become the Voice of Authority. Many of these have actually said, publicly, "It's easy to tell in the first week of art school who 'has it' and who doesn't. Those who don't, I try to discourage early."

There are also certain differences between true beginners, which have nothing to do with "inborn talent." A beginner who, for whatever reason, has spent years consciously observing people will have an advantage for a while over the beginner who paid no particular attention to people's physical appearances. It takes a long time for the human mind to consciously absorb such a large amount of detail. A similar example of unequal beginners is the one of beginners in a typing class: Most of the beginners are learning at about the same rate, but are amazed by one particular beginner whose rate of learning leaps incredibly beyond all the others'—until they find out that this particular beginner had been playing the piano for several years. Another difference is the simple fact that people's minds work differently, and so certain beginners' minds will be more compatible with a certain teacher's methods than another's.

An icy fear eventually grips the hearts of these older beginners, who are trying to "get through" the distasteful business of learning realistic figure drawing as quickly as

*Tex Avery's Droopy and the Wolf, plus an anonymous bull. Drawing, like throwing a bull, is impossible until you learn all the fundamentals. Then it's a breeze.* ©Loew's Incorporated

possible, and seem to be making such discouragingly slow progress. They ask themselves, "Am I untalented? Why can't I learn faster?"

Talent, to me, means the ability to learn and acquire skill, and a capacity for creativity which comes from a genuine love of an art form. To me the word does not mean some magical "gift" that only a lucky few are born with. (On the other hand, if talent is some innate predisposition toward art, it is probably that very predisposition that has caused such a deep love for art; in other words, the latter indicates the presence of the former. But in any case, all beginners start at the same place and go down the same path. The ones with the deeper love think about it all the time, and advance down the path in every possible moment; the ones with a lesser love advance down the path only occasionally, when it conveniently fits into an otherwise busy schedule.)

There are a few rare exceptions: certain physical or mental handicaps would impair a person's skills. For example, a person born tone deaf would probably not make a great musician, especially on the violin. A person born color blind might produce great black-and-white artwork but would probably never be a great colorist. A few rare people have an impaired mental process in which the brain does not properly process visual information. When I first entered the animation industry as an inbetweener, I met a fellow inbetweener (who later left the business) who seemed to be, for lack of a better word, shape blind (he possibly had dyslexia). Between two simple extremes of parallel concave lines, he would, as often as not, draw a convex line. Obviously he would have extreme difficulty as a draftsman, at least as long as his mental process

remained uncorrected. (At the opposite extreme, a person born with a photographic memory would obviously have a certain advantage, although there is more to being a creative artist than possessing even a perfect memory.)

"Why can't I learn faster?" One reason is that a drawing of a human figure involves far more complex details than the conscious mind can deal with. The conscious mind can retain only two or three new things at a time, which it attempts to pass on to the memory, in the subconscious mind. But the subconscious mind evidently disseminates new information to several different locations, which means that in any one location the intellectual impression is so weak that the conscious mind has to reinforce the impression with a certain amount of repetition. Furthermore, the memory has a greater ability to retain new information if it is associated with related knowledge, so that it is hardest to remember new information that is completely unfamiliar, but in time the learning process gets easier because the more you already know, the more you have available in the memory to associate new information with.

We get frustrated when we cannot copy onto paper an image that we can see right in front of us. But humans are not photocopy machines. Our hands draw not what our eyes see, but what our *minds* see. And the mind "sees" only as much as it *understands*. People assume that the mind sees through the eyes, but it does not. (A 1987 documentary, *The Brain,* aired on PBS Television describes this in detail.) The brain is blind—it "sees" only with its own understanding, its own comprehension. This, in turn, is taken from information *through* the eyes, and *through* the conscious mind, into the subconscious mind. For the mind to be most effective, it needs to be fully "programed," almost like a computer.

This mental process has to compensate for yet another oddity: In most cases, the more *accurate* we are in copying (as a line drawing) a real person, the worse the copy looks. For example, take a photo of a human in a magazine or newspaper, and *trace* the photo as a line drawing. The more accurate the tracing, the worse it will look. But a skilled (knowledgeable) draftsman will make many tiny changes, which will result in a drawing that looks more like the image in the photo than the tracing. This is primarily because a line drawing is, unavoidably, an extreme simplification—and therefore more of a graphic *symbol*. (In other words, a line drawing is not a complete visual reproduction like a painting, with all the three-dimensional shapes represented in light and shadow.)

People learn best through their emotions. For some reason, the memory retains an emotionally charged experience much more vividly than a predominantly intellectual experience. For the beginner who has no interest—who takes no emotional pleasure—in learning the human figure, the best advice may be to first eliminate the negative experiences: the frustrations of failure to meet goals set too high. In the beginning, do not attempt to make good drawings of the figure; instead, practice stick-figure proportions, eight heads tall, standing, sitting, and in action poses (referring to the how-to-draw books for information on proportions). Later, begin committing to memory, in diagram form rather than as attempts at finished drawings, the positions of bones and muscles, and their general (simplified) shapes—from all angles, and with the body both standing straight and in action poses. It takes a lot of time to memorize that many details, but slowly it'll start to happen. Draw, in diagram form, the individual features of the head—noses, ears, lips, eyes—to get acquainted with their complex shapes. In time, as your diagram stick figures become more familiar, they'll start to get more interesting.

Eventually, the diagram stick figures will begin to evolve into simplified drawings. This is the time to look for ways to make the experience fun. Myself, I found copying the straight illustration figures in the how-to-draw books—and the models in the life drawing classes—to be much too boring, at least in the beginning. I maintained my interest by first copying the more exaggerated, cartoony Wallace Wood drawings, from his work in the old 1950s *Mad* Magazines, and later graduated to Frazetta, Vargas, and finally Michelangelo.

One particular experience I had in a life drawing class is worth a special mention. I was drawing from an undraped model, trying to copy as accurately as I could, and my drawing was the most boring-looking thing—much like the model herself—and the instructor came over and offered to sit down and show me how to improve it. He made a vastly better drawing; he was copying the model's pose, but he was also idealizing the model's body by articulating—from his own knowledge of human anatomy—slight surface shapes of the placements of the bones and muscles. Plainly, he was drawing shapes that did not exist on the surface of the model. I asked him what the point was of drawing from a model, if a person is mainly drawing shapes from memory of information in anatomy books. His answer was, "Drawing out of your head gets repetitious; the poses that a model takes will be much more varied and show new possibilities (of twists and turns of the human form). The point is not to just copy the model, but to incorporate what you've learned about anatomy." This is what Michelangelo's drawings articulate so superbly well.

*A beautifully drawn Bugs Bunny in military uniform. This publicity drawing hints at the possibility of an interesting character and an adult storyline.* ©Warner Bros. Cartoons, Inc.

# III. LEARNING TO ANIMATE

New recruits to the animation industry are required only to know how to draw, and even if they do know a little about how to animate they will be started at the bottom of the animation ladder, as "inbetweeners." However, advancement will depend on how well the new people perform on the boards as draftsmen and how quickly they learn the skills of animation, so it is advantageous to learn as much about animation as possible prior to entering the studios. Like drawing, learning the basics of animation early—action analysis of walks and runs, balance in motion, overlapping actions—will allow a person to begin absorbing by osmosis a familiarity with the subtleties of human movements and gestures in daily life.

The goal of good animation is to convey *feeling*. Anything that moves is an action, and can be *seen* as such. But an animated action is good only if it has a feeling—of weight, of looseness, of balance-in-motion. Plus a *feeling*, from the way a character moves, of that character's emotions, whether he is hesitant or confident, of his energy or fatigue, of what he's thinking.

Animation classes in schools and universities, almost without exception, are able to teach only the mechanics of film making, and to introduce the students to the physical tools of the animation industry. They are not able to teach the students how to breathe life into drawn characters through animation. Fortunately, there are three very

excellent books available on the subject of how to animate. *Animation* and *How To Animate Film Cartoons,* both by Preston Blair, #26 and #190, respectively, in the Walter Foster art book series, $4.95 each, are sold in most art supply stores. These two books contain a lot of information on classical animation, by a top animator of the Disney and M.G.M. studios. (Sometime in the near future Preston Blair will combine these two books in a hardback edition, with several new pages which he is creating now.) *Disney Animation: The Illusion of Life* by Frank Thomas and Ollie Johnston, 1981, Abbeville Press, $39.95 (hardback) is a very extensive work on how to animate and how to make Disney-style animated films. Thomas and Johnston are two of the supervising animators who were known as "The Nine Old Men" of the Disney Studio.

Studying professional animation films frame by frame—in "stop motion"—is probably the best way to learn how many different kinds of cartoon action are handled, drawing by drawing. But be aware that in the current age of home video, there are a few technical obstacles. All professional motion picture films run at a speed of twenty-four frames per second, and all professional animation is timed for that speed and recorded on film (including cartoons made for television). However, all U. S. television (broadcast and home video) plays movies and TV shows at thirty frames per second. Consequently, film frames are broadcast on television, and recorded on videotape, in odd combinations. I have seen different variations of combinations of frames on different videotapes that were recorded on people's home videotape recorders and played back in the "still-frame-advance" mode; this makes single-framing in playback confus-

*Books recommended for the study of animation.*

ing insofar as knowing exactly how many frames of film a particular action took, especially considering a peculiarity of animation: In theatrical full animation, some actions (usually faster actions) are normally shot "on ones," which means there is a new drawing for every frame of film, and some actions (usually slower actions) are normally shot "on twos," which means that, usually for economic reasons, each drawing is shot on two consecutive frames of film. There are a few eccentric actions that actually look better "on twos" (or even "on threes") than "on ones," and many times a certain action will be shot partly on ones and partly on twos, for artistic rather than economic reasons.

Luckily for animation study purposes, nearly all professionally pre-recorded videotapes are recorded with a consistent pattern of one video frame for every film frame plus one extra video frame for every fourth film frame; in other words, film frames are recorded on these videotapes as 1-2-3-<u>4-4</u>-5-6-7-<u>8-8</u>-9-10-11-<u>12-12</u>-13-14-15-<u>16-16</u>-17-18-19-<u>20-20</u>-21-22-23-<u>24-24</u> et cetera. Most current television broadcasting seems to follow this same pattern, and many recent home videotape recorders accurately record this pattern.

Better yet are the laser videodiscs. Laser videodiscs recorded in the CLV "extended play" format are recorded in the 1-2-3-4-4 pattern described above, and although this format was not originally intended for single-frame playback, the more recent (and higher priced) laserdisc players can single-frame these discs, and single-frame advance both forward and backward. However, the laser videodiscs recorded in the CAV "stan-

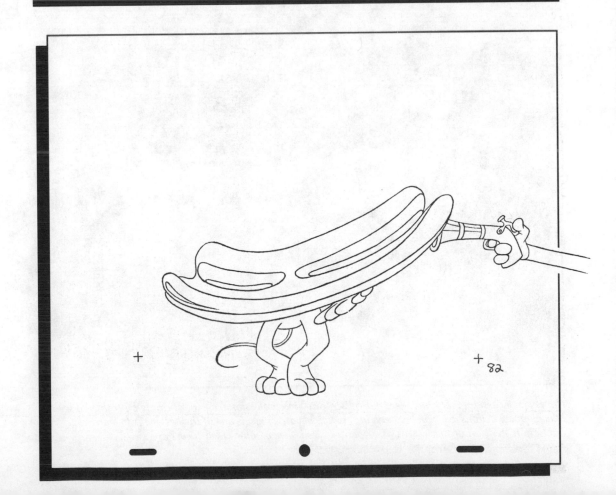

*Home video cassette tapes and laser videodiscs. Studying professional cartoons frame-by-frame, to see how complex actions are broken down into individual drawings, is one of the best ways to learn animation. All Warner Bros., M-G-M, Superman, and Disney home video covers are* ©Turner Entertainment Co, Turner Entertainment Co, Image Entertainment Inc, and The Walt Disney Company, respectively.

dard play" format (which was always intended to include single-frame playback) are recorded *entirely one video frame for each film frame*. The laserdisc *player* makes the necessary frame-compensations when playing the CAV disc at normal speed, but in single-frame playback of the CAV disc there is *no* confusion regarding how many frames of film any particular action took. (Note: These days, most live action titles on laser videodisc are recorded in the CLV format only.)

Unlike videotape, which stretches or wrinkles when single-framed often, thereby acquiring glitches in the picture, the laser videodisc can be single-framed often and for any length of time without wear. And because the laser videodisc is based on the same technology as the compact disc, more and more CD players now also play the laser videodiscs.

Occasionally a title goes out of print on the laser videodisc, just as a title sometimes does on videotape, but since a laser videodisc is far less susceptible to damage than videotape, some stores will buy and sell used (out-of-print) laser videodiscs. Such stores usually advertise in The Laser Disc Newsletter, which can be purchased or subscribed to from Suite 428, 496A Hudson Street, New York N.Y. 10014.

Several of the Disney feature length theatrical cartoons released on home video (including the laser videodisc, in both the CAV and CLV formats) contain elaborate effects animation such as water splashes, fire, smoke, et cetera. Few animation studios maintain reference material on effects, yet the animators are expected to animate them. Thus the Disney effects scenes are particularly valuable for reference.

The best way to acquire skills in animation is to animate various actions (in pencil) and shoot them, on film or videotape, and play them back at normal speed. This is called a "pencil test," and it is an infinitely more certain way to judge the accuracy of your timing than flipping the drawings in your hands. Single-frame video camera/recorders designed to shoot animation pencil tests, by the way, shoot on the basis of twenty four drawings per second, and automatically make compensated video recordings of each drawing, to play back at video speed without speeding up the animation timing. The advantage of the single-frame video recorders, of course, is the instant availability of playback, allowing the animator to make changes in his animation and shoot new pencil tests as many times as he likes in a short time—as opposed to waiting hours or days for a single film test to be developed. Most animation schools should have either film or video equipment for pencil testing, but if you have no access to an animation school, the least expensive pencil test equipment to buy would be a super-8mm camera that can shoot single-frame, and a super-8mm projector that runs at twenty four frames per second. Do not practice animation at the "home movie" speed of eighteen frames per second—that will teach a sense of timing that will have to be unlearned before you can animate professionally.

Good animation, like good cartooning, must ultimately be drawn from a knowledge of real action. Live action footage of baseball players is especially useful for study by single-framing, because baseball playing involves walking, running, sliding, jumping, throwing, falling down and getting up. Two books of sequential action photo-

*Most laser videodiscs are recorded in the CLV "extended play" format, but laserdiscs with covers displaying the CAV ("standard play") label are recorded with one video frame for each film frame, which is better for studying animation frame-by-frame. Some laserdisc titles, including most of the Disney feature length cartoons, are available in both CLV and CAV formats.* © The Walt Disney Company

graphs by Eadweard Muybridge, *The Human Figure in Motion* and *Animals in Motion* ($22.95 each, Dover Press), are helpful, but the photographs were made by a series of still cameras (back in the late 1800s), and the increments of elapsed time between the cameras are not quite even, so the books can be a little misleading in the exact timing of the actions (plus, of course, the cameras were not timed for twenty-four pictures per second).

Some surprising discoveries will be made while studying live action footage frame by frame, such as observing how fast the real human body can move, and how distorted it can become in fast or violent actions—plus how distorted the single frame-photos of the human body become in certain fast actions, even at twenty-four photos (frames) per second. From such discoveries as these, some of the Warner cartoon directors and animators learned how far they could exaggerate and distort their drawings for comic effect—in fact, they had to distort some of their character drawings literally beyond recognition (usually for only one or two frames at a time, before returning to normal) to achieve the effect of fluid, wild exaggeration of action; particularly good examples of this are in some of the mid-1940s Warner cartoons directed by Bob Clampett, such as *Baby Bottleneck* (1945) and *Kitty Kornered* (1946). Of course, live action footage, in spite of how extreme and distorted some of the individual frames are, looks very normal when run at standard projection speed, and the Disney animators, at Walt's insistence, learned from the live action footage how to make their animation feel broad and loose and still seem natural and restrained.

*The classic 1940s version of M-G-M's Tom and Jerry.* ©Loew's Incorporated

The advantages and importance of studying live action footage frame by frame cannot be over-emphasized. However, a professional animator will need to know even more than the mechanics of real motion. He should study actors and books on acting. It is also advisable to know staging, choreography, dance steps, and the principles of music (animation, for artistic effect, is occasionally organized similarly to music, with all of its rhythm, counterpoint, etc.).

Animation timing is at least as vast a subject to learn and practice as drawing. The best animation, in the actual timing of its details of motion, is not figured out in the head, by thinking it out. The conscious mind cannot deal with matters that complex. It has to be *felt*, which is the domain of the subconscious mind. But for the subconscious mind to be effective, it must have the basic knowledge already fed into it through the conscious mind.

Animating well, like drawing well, is an act of expressing a feeling about an action (of a character). Ideally, to achieve fluidity in animation, the animator will first draw (in animation) the *motion* (the force, the sweep of action), then draw the figure doing the motion, bending and turning and stretching the figure to fit the motion. (This need not imply that the figure becomes rubbery.) Art Babbitt—another of the top Disney animators from the classic era, and later an excellent animation instructor—in his action analysis lectures, often stressed, "You learn the rules (of action analysis), then you *break* the rules—you animate your *impression*."

By far the most difficult action to learn to animate is a realistic human walk cycle. The reason, of course, is that people are so familiar with human walk actions from seeing them so frequently in daily life that the slightest error (in the animation) is immediately sensed; plus the fact that the average human walk action is so full of subtle, complex motions (involving body weight distribution and balance-in-motion) that a realistic depiction of it requires the most extreme accuracy in every line and detail. If a character (or a person in real life) is doing something—anything—while he is walking, it affects the delicate interacting internal balance of the walk, making a slightly awkward walk look perfectly normal—which frees the animator from the necessity of such extreme precision. However, the knowledge of a "straight" realistic human walk action is the basis for the quality of invention of all other walk cycles. And, unavoidably, every animator at some time or other gets a scene that requires a very "straight," literal human walk—and so it has proven to be not only the most difficult but also the most important action to learn to animate.

Every beginner's first reaction to the problem of animating a realistic human walk is, "Why not rotoscope it?"—that is, why not shoot it in live action and simply trace the (projected or enlarged) frames of live action film? For some reason, the results of rotoscoping are invariably unsatisfying, much as a line drawing of a person's face is unsatisfying when traced from a photograph. In each case, a slight degree of interpretation—or "amplification"—is needed to make the drawing look right or the action (of a drawing) feel right. Achieving just the right kind of "amplification" requires a very complete knowledge of a real walk action.

Surprisingly, none of the books on animation listed above, or any other published sources that I've ever found, has articulated the details of a "straight" realistic human walk action. (Actually, some of the transcripts in the Disney Studio archives of the action analysis lectures given by Don Graham at the Disney Studio in the mid to late 1930s address the problem with great thoroughness, but the lectures were accompa-

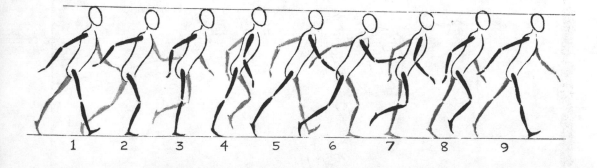

1    2    3    4    5    6    7    8    9

© *Preston Blair Productions, from his book* **How to Animate Film Cartoons**, *page 29.*

nied at the time by projections of frames of live action film; without access to those frames of film, it is almost impossible to deduce from the transcripts just what Don Graham was referring to.)

To better understand the principles of a basic walk of a realistic human figure, compare the first four "plates" in the Muybridge book, *The Human Figure in Motion* (listed above, in this chapter), with the profile walk of the diagramed human figure at the top of page 29 in Preston Blair's book, *How to Animate Film Cartoons* (book #190). The walk cycle in the Blair book appears to be of a man in a great hurry; compared to an average walk, the body here is leaning much farther forward, the arms are swinging much too high, and the legs and feet are pretty much the way they would be except that the foot coming off the ground lifts up too high in the air. Preston Blair evidently felt that such an exaggerated walk cycle would "read" better—that is, be easier for the student to see and understand on the single printed page. In a normal "average" walk, the arms would move forward and back only a little, the head and body would move up and down only about one eighth the height of the head, and the body would be considerably more upright.

Number the drawings of the walk cycle in the Blair book, from left to right—1, 2, 3, 4, 5, 6, 7, 8, 9. On the first drawing (the "contact," or "hit" drawing), in a normal walk the figure's chin would be directly above the space *between* the two feet, at about three quarters the distance forward from the toe of the back foot to the heel of the front foot. On the second drawing (the "catching the weight" drawing), the figure's

chin would be directly over the heel of the forward foot (in the profile view only—not in a "front view," obviously). Also, on the second drawing, the forward leg wouldn't bend (or "crouch") quite that much in a normal walk. In the third drawing (the "figure four" drawing, so-called because in profile—especially when the character is facing the opposite direction—the straight leg and the bent leg resemble a numeral figure four), the figure's chin would be over the toe of the forward foot. And so on. Compare these notes with the photographs in the Muybridge book, and especially with your observation of real people walking.

These rules alone are enough for a decent first practice test. If you add one "inbetween" drawing between each of the drawings indicated in this cycle in the Blair book—so that you now have 1, 1A, 2, 2A, 3, etc.—and then shoot all of these drawings on "twos"—that is, expose each of the drawings on two consecutive frames of film— you will have a total of sixteen frames of film per step, which is the right amount of screen time for a casual walk. Only by shooting such a pencil test can you see how close you are to what you want, and then it is much easier to judge what (relatively minor) changes to make. For example, the person's stride (per step) might be slightly farther or shorter, his passing foot may lift slightly higher or lower off the ground, and so forth.

Keeping track of all the positions of the arms and legs and the up and down of the body—drawing by drawing by drawing—is very complicated and confusing for any beginner. After you have animated such walks several times (and pencil tested them), only then will they become familiar enough in your mind that your attention will be freed to concentrate on the refinements of the walk action which will make it more fluid and less mechanical.

Some of the refinements of the human walk action are: Just as the arms and legs counter each other forward and back to maintain body balance (as the left leg moves forward, the left arm moves back), the hips and shoulders also move (a little bit)

*Bottom of page 28 in Preston Blair's book #190.  © Preston Blair Productions, from his book* **How to Animate Film Cartoons**, *page 28.*

forward and back to follow the direction of the arms and legs (the arms and legs are not just thumb-tacked onto a block of wood). The hips and shoulders also counter each other up and down (see bottom of page 28 of Blair's book #190 as well as the middle of its back cover) to maintain body balance—the hip moves up on the side supporting the body weight, while the opposite hip drops down, and the left shoulder drops down as the left hip moves up, and so on. Remember that these (slight) up and down, and forward and back, movements of the shoulders and hips can be articulated in the profile view as well as the front view. You may have to exaggerate these actions on the first few practice tests, to fix this jumble of opposing actions clearly in your mind, but later they will start to become familiar and you can articulate them more subtly, to achieve a more realistic action.

The wrists "break" when the arms change direction—that is, as the arm is moving forward, the hand is dragging back, and when the arm reaches its extreme forward position the hand is still in the dragging back position, but on the next drawing, in which the arm is starting to move back, the hand pivots slightly upward at the wrist, now trailing in the other direction. Sort of like a cloth rag at the end of a stick. In like manner, the back foot drags back as the back leg starts to move forward; the foot changes its direction slower than the leg does as the leg lifts forward and up, and the foot doesn't actually flip upward until the "contact" drawing, in which the heel hits the ground. These are simply "overlapping" actions, which add a feeling of looseness to the overall action, and which do occur in real life. The same is true of all drapery—sleeves,

pant legs, coat tails, flowing skirts and dresses—and hair, which drops back as the body moves up and then fluffs up slightly as the body moves down.

Note also that as the paths of the hands dip in an arc as the arms and hands move forward and back (see text on left side of page 29 in the Blair book #190), the paths of the hands also swing in a slight arc around the sides of the body (somewhat like a tether ball swinging around a pole) as the hands and arms move forward and back.

When the human figure is walking on a "pan" background—that is, when the figure is walking in place (in profile), as if on a treadmill, while the background moves past the camera—the refinements of the walk cycle are even more important, as ways to break up the monotony of absolute symmetry. One area of refinement is to look for legitimate ways to turn the hands and feet slightly towards and away from camera as they reach the extremes of their forward-and-back movements. For example, on page 29 in the Blair book again, in the cycle walk that we numbered 1 through 9, on the back foot of drawing one we would show a little of the sole of the shoe, and on the back foot of drawing five we would show more of the front of the shoe. Another area is to let the body gain forward just slightly on the pan on drawings 1, 5, and 9, and lose back slightly on the pan on drawings 3 and 7 (with the remaining drawings between those positions); that slight forward and back motion of the body, combined with the up and down of the body during the walk cycle, gives the body a slightly circular motion, in a clockwise direction. This circular motion should not be broad enough to be noticeable, but just enough so that the lines of half of the drawings in each cycle don't coincide exactly on the same place on the screen.

So far we've been talking about walk cycles timed at sixteen film frames per step, but another very standard walk cycle is one timed at twelve frames per step. Back to page 29 of Blair's book again, we use fewer inbetweens—specifically, we make an inbetween only between drawings 2 and 3, 4 and 5, 6 and 7, and 8 and 9—and shoot that on twos. This is the right amount of screen time for a normal walk of a person who is not rushed but has a serious intent of going somewhere. (Of course, in drawings 2, 4, 6, and 8 the positions of the feet on the ground have to be shifted slightly so that the spacing between the feet on the ground of all the drawings will be even.) This very standard walk, however, has a standard peculiar problem: on drawings 3, 4, and 4A the leg coming forward is bent; on drawing 5 the leg goes straight out to touch the ground; on drawing 6 the leg bends forward to cushion the body weight. The problem is the positions of the knee: the knee has progressed forward up to drawing 4A, dropped back on drawing 5, which is okay, but on drawing 6 the knee has jumped forward again, beyond its position in drawing 5—which on the screen looks like a drawing of the knee (either number 5 or 6) has popped out of place—it looks like a mistake. The same peculiar action does occur in real life too, if you watch a friend's knees carefully as he walks at a moderately fast pace. The only solution to this peculiarity seems to be, on drawing 6, to cheat slightly on the physical length of the leg, to bend the knee forward as little as possible. (The leg in drawing 5 has to be completely straight, or the action will look strange, a little bit like a Groucho Marx crouch-walk.)

An action that is not noticeable in a profile walk (and therefore is not of concern to the animator), but which is noticeable in any other view of a walk, such as a front view or a three-quarter view, is the tendency for the body to shift its weight slightly from side to side, depending on which foot is on the ground and supporting the body weight. Watch people walking toward you in real life, to see how slight but how noticeable this is. A related action is a very slight tendency for the trunk of the body to bend and twist with each step—not nearly as much in real life as shown on bottom of page 28 in the Blair book, but something on that order.

One aside to keep in mind about getting extra weight in a walk: a heavy man will remain in the crouched, "catching the weight," bent-leg position about two frames longer than a man of average weight. This affects the timing of the whole walk cycle: the total number of frames may be the same (for example), but the heavy man's body will lift up slower (more of the drawings in the cycle, advancing upward), and drop down faster (fewer drawings in the cycle, moving downward).

After you've animated many more walk cycles (and pencil tested them), incorporating the refinements mentioned above, you will probably have developed a genuine interest in watching people in real life more closely—and studying live action film closer, frame by frame—to look for different kinds of walks to animate, and caricature and exaggerate. In your practicing, don't forget that in full animation you will very likely get a scene requiring you to animate a character walking around a corner, or even around in a full circle. Humans running, and four-legged animals walking and running, and large-winged birds flying all require quite a lot of study and practice, and perhaps ought to be approached in the same manner as that suggested in chapter two about how to endure the training period of learning to draw the realistic human figure. But once mastered, these skills will allow you an enormous freedom to explore new ideas in dramatic or funny new ways.

*Pecos Bill and his horse Widowmaker, beautifully designed cartoon human and cartoon horse, incorporating lots of strong yet elegant geometric shapes. From Disney's **Melody Time** (1948).*
©Walt Disney Productions

# PART TWO:
# ELEVATING THE ART FORM

# IV. RE-DEFINING THE MEDIUM

Animated cartoon: A style of humorous or dramatic representation, often caricaturing or distorting the characters, their environments and motion, to show how things look emotionally in the mind of the perceiver, as opposed to how things look to the physical eye. Artistically, cartoon films can be—and should be—as different from live action as paintings are from photography.

The future of animation is as good as a team of writer, producer, and designer-animator would want to make it. And that is precisely the problem: it does require at least three people of such different professional skills to work together, in mutual agreement on a common goal, just to create and sell a new idea for a film of any respectable, commercial and artistic significance. The vast majority of films that the cartoon industry produces today are very poor, but not because good animated films are too expensive to make; in fact, the cost of shooting live action has increased so rapidly in the past two decades that the cost of cartoon animation compares very favorably. Animation's sorry condition was brought on instead by a lack of established producers who truly wanted to achieve something significant with the art form, and especially by the virtual absence in the field of writers whose work is as good as that of the best screenwriters in live action. There has been virtually no serious emotional adult content in the writing for most animated films; animation studios have consis-

tently rejected top professional writers, operating on the assumption that sight gags are animation's only viable stock-in-trade. As a result, the writing for most animated films has become embarrassingly juvenile.

Good intentions, by themselves, are not enough. In the past several years, whenever someone from the animation ranks with good intentions has obtained financial backing to make an animated film, they have invariably grossly underestimated the value of a good story and the need to hire a good writer. Instead, operating on the erroneous yet widespread assumption that no live action screen writer or novelist could possibly write as well for a cartoon film as an artist, since (supposedly) only an artist or animator really understands the animation medium, they attempt to fake their way (in a few weeks) through writing a story, claiming that the great artwork will make up for any weaknesses that the story may have. But it just never works. It's the equivalent of trying to improve a bad novel by hand-lettering every word in old gothic.

A large number of individuals in the animation industry over the past several years have shared an intense, desperate desire to somehow write, produce and animate profoundly beautiful cartoon films that would excite the imaginations of the industry and the public alike, and which would be so financially successful that animators could continue expanding their artistic horizons for decades to come. These people look back with high admiration and aching envy at the Disney Studio's greatest achievements— *Snow White, Pinocchio, Fantasia, Bambi*—all produced between 1936 and 1942—and

*Brom Bones and Ichabod Crane in Disney's **The Legend of Sleepy Hollow** (1949). Even though Brom Bones is the "handsome suitor" in the story, he is still a cartoon design rather than a more literal illustration.* ©Walt Disney Productions

many of these people today wish they could have been around in those days to have just been a part of that creative environment. (Similarly, many of these people also look back at the greatest achievements of the other studios in their theatrical shorts of the 1940s and early 1950s, although—since movie theaters no longer rent shorts, and since there is not yet a comparable new marketplace for shorts—most of the serious attention today is turned to the possibilities of making good theatrical features.)

The most common mistake such people make, however, is to want to emulate the classic Disney films too closely, without realizing that theater audiences of today are vastly different from those of the late 1930s or even of the 1950s, when Disney did his second-best series of cartoon features. What might have been commercially successful in Disney's day is not necessarily what will succeed today. As time goes by, the public's tastes change, its interests change—and political climates, which have a strong influence on people's attitudes, also change.

Even in Disney's day, Disney's best features were not always successful. Luckily, his first feature, *Snow White and the Seven Dwarfs* (1937), was a fantastic commercial success—partly because it was such a novelty, and partly because it was the right choice of subject at the right time, released while America (and Europe) was still in the Great Depression (which motivated movie audiences to embrace escapist fantasy so overwhelmingly). But Disney's next three major features following *Snow White*— *Pinocchio* (1940), *Fantasia* (1940) and *Bambi* (1942)—had much of the same emotional tones as *Snow White*, yet all lost money in their first release. By 1940, the

American public's attention was turned to the growing threat of war, and so the public mood was very different from what it had been in 1937 and 1938. The authorized Disney Studio histories point out that part of the reason for the lack of financial success for those three features was that the war in Europe cut off the European theatrical marketplace. But that would also have been true for all the Hollywood movie companies, yet the live action motion picture industry made more money in the 1940s, both during and after World War Two, than at any other time in history (taking into account the relative value of 1940s dollars). The authorized Disney Studio histories also state that there was a certain unwillingness on the part of theaters to book a Disney feature length cartoon because they played largely to children, whose tickets sold for less money, while the theaters could make more money by running movies that appealed more to adult audiences. The only big theatrical cartoon hit Disney had in the 1940s was *Dumbo* (1941), which at least proved that a cartoon could stand a chance.

Today, with television in almost every home, the movie theaters are no longer frequented by all age groups, as they were before TV. Instead, the movies are attended almost exclusively by the high school and college-age crowd. Understanding who the theater audience is today, and what its tastes and prejudices are, is absolutely crucial to achieving a commercial success. The purpose of this book, then, (especially in chapter five, on writing for animation) forces me to have to play devil's advocate to try to

*Peter Pan is closer to being an illustration than the more cartoony Chief. In other Disney films, including* **Cinderella** *and* **Sleeping Beauty***, the lead characters are almost literal illustration figures resembling live photography.* ©Walt Disney Productions

demonstrate how today's young adults—the theater audience—looks at even the best animated films from the present and past, and how to guess what they might prefer to see.

For years the standards for most of the animation industry were established by the Walt Disney Studio. Disney, throughout most of his career, was seeking to achieve respectability in the art and film communities, and he put all of his emphasis on the "believability" and naturalism of the drawings and animation, always looking over his shoulder at the achievements of the live action comedians of his day. This single-minded emphasis brought his animated films ever closer to the constraining literalism of live-action photography, and probably had a lot to do with the formation of the erroneous beliefs that animation's only advantage over the believability of live action lay in the area of pure fantasy—subject matter largely impossible to film in live action—and that fantasy is primarily a children's domain.

More recent years have seen a spate of feature-length theatrical cartoons, including several by Ralph Bakshi, that were publicized as containing adult material; despite a few R and X ratings, none of them rose much above the level of adolescent vulgarities. The writing in these films—including the "screen adaptations" in the cases of films based on respectable books—was so trite that it would never have been accepted by any self-respecting live action film producer or director.

For all these reasons, animated cartoons have acquired a dismal reputation, particularly during the past three decades. Yet I contend that this is not due to inher-

*Tony and Joe, from Disney's **Lady and the Tramp**, are particularly well drawn and animated cartoon humans, with lots of expressive "dialog" animation as they serenade.* ©Walt Disney Productions

ent limitations of the medium. One area—unfortunately, the only area—that anima-tion film makers have explored in depth is that of slapstick comedy. The best cartoon theatrical shorts of the late 1930s—and especially the best of the Warner cartoons (Bugs Bunny, Daffy Duck, etc.) of the 1940s*—caused great concern among live-action comedians because no matter what kinds of sight gags the comedians tried, the car-toons could do them better, with more exaggeration and with sharper timing—and with a high degree of believability. In this area, the cartoon film makers matched, and topped, live action—but on their own terms, by exploring the unique possibilities of drawings over photographs, and of animation (artificially created motion) over live action.

The animated cartoon film with an adult dramatic narrative is very difficult to describe because it has scarcely been attempted; it is an art form waiting to be born, containing possibilities almost entirely unexplored and unknown. This is strange when one considers how long we have accepted more adult themes in newspaper political cartoons, and cartoons in adult magazines such as the *Saturday Evening Post, Playboy* and *The New Yorker*.

*Most of the Warner cartoons shown on television, especially network programs, are the ones made in the 1950s, which are very pale attempts compared to the ones of the 1940s, and are therefore not much of an example of the point being made here.

*Another view of Pecos Bill and Widowmaker, from Disney's **Melody Time**.* ©Walt Disney Productions

What might a writer or director want to study, to try to explore the artistic and dramatic possibilities of an adult cartoon (as different from adult live action films)? A broad answer is, any possible ways of combining good adult fiction with its visual equivalent—in non-literal imagery—in mood and tone. Probably theater stage design and twentieth century art, especially the expressionist movement, and realistic American painters in the vein of Edward Hopper. (Incidentally, my experience has been that good picture books on stage design graphics are difficult to find. You may have to do some looking around in special-interest book stores, used book stores and specialized libraries.)

A potential advantage of drawings over photographs is the ease with which they can distort, caricature and exaggerate; this applies to shapes, colors and motion. The total film—not just the characters—can be as fluid as dance. Images can flow like a dream—and "dream" doesn't necessarily mean fantasy. It can mean a non-literal stream-of-consciousness, someone's *perception* of reality.

Looking to live action films for inspiration is tricky, because to the extent that the films are well conceived, they are such vivid examples of "how live action does it best" that they obscure any suggestion of how to do it differently in animation. However, the more recent live action theatrical films and the better live action television commercials should be studied for their increasingly sophisticated use of film "language": cuts, jump cuts, dissolves, overlapping of sound and picture, zooming, freeze frame, et cetera. Tomorrow's theatrical cartoons should maintain a similar degree of sophistica-

tion or risk looking old hat and amateur.

Among animated films, examples of sophisticated visual dramatic possibilities are fragmentary at best. A limited-animation theatrical cartoon from U.P.A., *The Tell-Tale Heart* (1953), by Ted Parmelee and Paul Julian, based on the famous story by Edgar Allan Poe, is a good example of an application of twentieth century art and/or stage design to the medium of the animated film. (*The Tell-Tale Heart* is available on video tape, in a collection titled, "Columbia Cartoon Classics Vol. 9.") In Ralph Bakshi's heavily flawed *Heavy Traffic* (1973), there is an interesting sequence near the end of the film in which Angelo (Michael's father), in a drunken stupor, seeks audience with the mafia godfather; this sequence is quite surreal, both in drawing and writing, and represents Angelo's drunken, terrified perception of this encounter. (*Heavy Traffic* is also available on video tape.) The last twenty minutes of *Bambi* (1942) are probably Disney's most interpretive piece of dramatic narrative; the lighting and environment change radically, underscoring Bambi's internal emotions as he falls in love with Faline, is bullied into a stag fight, and "hears" the romance of the windsong in the moonlit meadow.

As if attempting to identify the elements of a commercially successful cartoon film to a writer isn't difficult enough, raising the money to hire a writer can prove to be a real Catch 22, since the story—along with good professional credentials as a potential cartoon film maker—is usually the key prerequisite for acquiring financial backing in the first place. In deciding your career, it may be that you should spend a few years learning how to write, or team up with another cartoon enthusiast who is willing to learn to write while you learn how to draw, animate and direct. It could be well worth the effort—the process could snowball. Once a good cartoon story has been written and properly produced, it might attract the interest of some really great writers and conceptualists, who in turn (if allowed) could advance the art form beyond all of our dreams.

# V.   WRITING FOR ANIMATION

Writing is the most important single part of any successful theatrical film, because the writing—the "story"—is primarily what the public is interested in. Not the good animation.

Good animation, like good everything else, amounts to good production values which enhance an intelligent story.

The biggest problem today in attempting any decent writing in animation for adult audiences is trying to overcome the widespread, erroneous concept of what cartoons are "supposed to be," based on what cartoons have always been: primarily children's fantasies, fairy tales, and slapstick sight gags (not to mention the mindless drek made for Saturday morning network television).

Perhaps the best way to write for animation is to take an adult situation—any adult situation—and caricature it. Either comedically or dramatically. We tend to think of comedy, like that of Woody Allen, when we think of caricature, but caricature can also convey a dramatic tone, as demonstrated in certain stage plays. Try to make the exposition more visual than verbal; avoid prolonged dialog unless there is an element of caricature in the way a character delivers his lines.

Animation film, like highly stylized stage theater, can capitalize on its ability to make images melt and flow from one scene to the next. Part of the fun of writing for

animation should be conceiving how to "play" the scenes like liquid visual music.

Inside the animation industry there is a widespread lack of comprehension of any difference between children's stories and adult stories, and this lack of comprehension seems to extend also to most of the people who aspire to get into the animation business. These people express shock and indignation when told that the old Disney cartoon feature classics are not adult; they can't understand that stories about lost puppies and baby elephants do not address adult concerns. Part of this mental conditioning comes from associating the subject matter of the older Disney cartoons with a very respectable quality of animation, and part of this mental conditioning comes from the deliberate reminders, in many of the Disney books on animation, of the association of fairy tales with old ballets and classical music—the stuff of high culture. (Again, I am very fond of some of the old Disney cartoon features; my intent here is to properly identify the subject matter, not to condemn it.)

Tone, of course, has a lot to do with how palatable a subject can be. The Warner cartoons used very much the same subject matter as Disney's, but the Warner cartoons usually contained a degree of sly adult wit; in many of the Disney cartoons, cloying cuteness predominated.

But to get an audience to respond deeply and enthusiastically, especially for ninety continuous minutes, the choice of subject is crucial. Most teenage and young adult movie-goers are primarily interested in stories that relate directly to their own immediate lives, or their most personal wish-fulfillment fantasies. This accounts for why adult fantasies often involve sex, romance, violence, get-rich-quick schemes, espionage and social climbing.

The audience should be able to recognize something of themselves in the central characters on the screen, or those characters should be the type of people that the audience would find interesting in real life.

Read widely the kinds of magazines the public reads, especially the news magazines, to develop a feeling for their interests—and also their political prejudices. Even though your choice of subject may not be a particular political issue, the political prejudices of the audience will color their attitudes towards every single element in your story. Successful advertising people and live action screenwriters are very aware of that. Today the movie-going public is not a single audience—it is fragmented into many different audiences, with different tastes and attitudes. One of the secrets of writing a successful movie is being aware of the attitudes of these different specific audiences and trying to appeal to as many of them as possible.

Where do story ideas come from? They come from real life situations. Don't just look at old cartoons; think back over your own past experiences, and watch carefully the people and situations around you. Try to figure out what motivates people to do what they do (as opposed to what they *say* their reasons are). Study psychology and sociology. Remember that "story" is more than plot and character; it is an exposition of our ever expanding comprehension of our human nature, and changing social mores.

If the last paragraph sounds too somber and serious, remember that the funniest comedy—at least to the largest number of people—is that which reflects real life experiences in some meaningful way.

"Impossible" gags can provide an interesting approach to an adult cartoon situation, as long as they reflect intense emotions that are "true to life." An example, of sorts, is the dramatic-comedic final sequence in Disney's *The Legend of Sleepy Hollow*

(1949) (available on video tape, although all the video tape copies I've seen have been uniformly too dark, obscuring a lot of the action and details; much better to see this cartoon on film). Unfortunately, most of the first half of this cartoon is silly to the point of being embarrassing, but the last ten minutes, of Ichabod's terror in the dark woods, is brilliant. This final sequence contains a collection of impossible gags, such as the one in which Ichabod, in his desperate attempt to avoid the Headless Horseman, grabs a tree and with his feet pulls his own horse off the ground in mid gallop and turns him around. Here the very impossibility of the gags expresses the intensity of Ichabod's desperation, and for that reason it all seems perfectly natural—and exhilarating.

Successful film writing depends also on understanding why people go to the theaters. A few important facts have been determined: the largest age group is college-age young adults who are dating, and the second largest age group is the high school students. They are going to the movies more for social reasons, and to get out of the house, than to see the movie itself. (After they get married and begin to raise a family, their theater attendance drops enormously.) To the extent that the movie-goers are interested in the movie itself, it is to have an intense emotional experience. Movies live or die on "word of mouth"—what people say to their friends about the movie they saw—so it is necessary to grab the audiences' attention early—to start with a bang, allow no dull spots in the body of the film, and end with an exciting climax, so that the audience leaves the theater on an emotional high, eager to tell their friends how great the movie was.

The best examples of commercially successful films to learn from, obviously, are the ones that have made the most money. Those are the movies that generated the strongest word of mouth and attracted the largest number of people. A list of feature length movies, in order of their theater box-office success, appears once each year in *Variety*, a weekly show business trade journal. (There is also a Daily Variety, from the same publisher, but it does not publish this list.) This list, updated annually, appears in *Variety's* special "American Film Market" issue, usually on or about the third Monday in February. The list includes with each title the year of release and the total amount of rental money paid to the film distributors by all of the movie theaters (a percentage of the box office gross) in the "domestic market," which is the United States and Canada. A particular value of the list, for example, is to compare the relative successes of different movies of a particular genre, such as comedies or action adventure films, and try to guess what made one film in that genre more successful than another film in the same genre. If you decide you want to write a musical, you will want to find out all you can about the contents and relative successes of all the other musicals. For subscription rates, write to: Weekly Variety, Subscription Department, 5700 Wilshire Blvd., Suite 120, Los Angeles, CA 90099-3253. Or check your local library.

Writing for animation involves the skills of good fiction writing in general. One might assume that one good book on how to write fiction would be sufficient, that two

*Ichabod and the Headless Horseman, from Disney's **The Legend of Sleepy Hollow**.* ©Walt Disney Productions

or more good books would tend to cover the same information. But the subject is so large that several excellent books deal each with a different facet of the subject and rarely overlap.

*Screenplay* by Syd Field, 1979, 1982, Dell Publishing, $8.95 (paperback) discusses the elements of screenwriting and emphasizes the basic plot structure, with its variations, for theatrical feature films, incorporating the more recent insights into the fundamental art of cinematic storytelling. Includes examples from some of the best live action films.

*Adventures in the Screen Trade* by William Goldman, 1983, Warner Books, $14.95 (paperback) gives a multitude of valuable insights into the screenwriter's intentions in the writing of each of several well-written live action screenplays (Goldman's own), and the reactions of theater audiences, both positive and negative. One of the central themes throughout the book is the attempt to analyze and understand what makes a commercially successful, respectable adult film story, especially as audience attitudes continue to change every year.

*On Becoming a Novelist* by John Gardner, 1983, Harper and Row, $13.95 (hardback), and *The Art of Fiction* by John Gardner, 1983, Alfred A. Knopf, $13.95 (hardback). These two books describe and compare all different genres of fiction, the kind of thinking and background necessary for good fiction writing, and how fiction emotionally affects the reader. The information here is applicable to film as well as literature, and the author—a very highly renowned teacher of creative writing—is comfortable

with the best of the popular arts as well as the highest traditions of literature.

*The Art of Dramatic Writing* by Lajos Egri, 1946, 1960, Simon and Schuster, $10.95 (paperback), emphasizes the structures of drama through character dialog.

*The Art of Creative Writing* by Lajos Egri, 1965, Citadel Press, $5.95 (paperback) explores the psychology of character types in dramatic situations.

*Taking It All In* by Pauline Kael, published 1984, Holt, Rinehart and Winston, $14.95 (large paperback) is a collection of film criticism by the prominent New York film critic, originally published in *The New Yorker* from 1980 to 1984. This and other collected works of film criticism are important, even if one does not always agree with the critic, because a good critic at least makes one think more carefully about character, tone, and all the other elements in the writing of films.

A good bookstore to know about is Larry Edmunds Bookshop, Inc., 6644 Hollywood Blvd., Hollywood, Calif., 90028. This bookstore specializes in books dealing with all facets of filmmaking, both in print and out of print, including books on screenwriting, directing, producing, and animation, and their collection of books and memorabilia on cinema is very complete. They respond to inquiries and they sell books by mail.

One last generality on screenwriting: There's an old saying that the most successful songs are love songs, and—keeping in mind the movie audiences, and the real reason they are in the theater—the vast majority of successful movies are either about,

*Recommended books on how to write for animation.*

or prominently include, a male-female romantic interest. This can be annoying when you want to do a ghost story, and it has to be a ghost story with a prominent romantic theme, or you want to do a science fiction film, and it has to be a science fiction film with a prominent romantic theme. But study the current and recent successful movies and notice how they work the romantic theme into every genre. (The most glaring exception, of course, is *E.T. The Extra-Terrestrial,* 1982, which is at the top of Variety's January 1990 list of domestic rental successes.)

*Freddie Moore (left) and Ward Kimball, two of the top animators at the Disney Studio, caricatured here in
drawing and animation by Ward Kimball in* **Nifty Nineties** *(1941), a Mickey Mouse short.*

# VI. DIRECTING ANIMATION FILMS

This entire book applies to cartoon film direction, because a cartoon film director ideally must be very knowledgeable about writing and producing, and very experienced as an animator. The director assumes the largest responsibility for the artistic success of a film, as he oversees and controls all stages of the film's production. Unlike most live action films, cartoon films are both conceived and edited in advance of actual animation production, right down to the single frame. An animation director needs the thorough knowledge of an animator to time out on paper not only the length of each scene, but all the individual bits of action correctly so as not to mislead the animators.

The director also needs to know at least a little about color, music, sound recording and voice casting, and a lot about staging, camera mechanics, and film "language": cuts, jump cuts, dissolves, overlapping of sound and picture, zooming, freeze-frame, et cetera. It is fully the director's responsibility to time and stage every scene in the picture in a way that will insure its maximum emotional impact and effectiveness.

There are many different styles and approaches to film direction, and they tend to be deeply personal to each director, which makes it very difficult to say what a director should or shouldn't do. In fact, what one director will virtually prove cannot be done at all on film, another director will accomplish with ease. There is some middle ground that can be commented on, however—examples of general pluses and minuses from

the history of the better theatrical cartoons. On the minus side are those directors who appear to have staged all their scenes exclusively for visual clarity, and to have regarded the camera as simply a recording device. There's nothing very exciting or imaginative about their films (except maybe the funny gags that their writers provided). Other directors have designed their films on much more cinematic terms, utilizing stylish cutting, unusual camera angles, and so forth, but with very little consideration about the characters of the story or the real concerns of those characters.

On the plus side, some directors think out their films from the point of view of not only visual clarity and interesting staging, but of also presenting the story and the characters in ways that will best articulate the characters' personalities and predica-

*Director Bob Clampett with story men Michael Sasanoff and Hubie Karp (both seated), and layout artist Tom McKimson (rear), in 1945. The storyboards are for* **The Big Snooze** *(left) and* **The Great Piggy Bank Robbery.** *(Notice the drawing of So White on the back wall.)*  ©Warner Bros. Cartoons, Inc.

ments. This alone accounts for most of the better work done in animated films to date. Obvious exceptions are some of Disney's stunningly beautiful set-pieces of "illustrated music"—such as *Clair de Lune* (1941) and *Bumble Boogie* (1948)—in which no limits were set on what might be presented on the screen.

But in the area of cinematic story-telling, probably the most exciting cartoon director to date was Bob Clampett, particularly for some of his wilder Warner cartoons of the mid 1940s, some of which include *Coal Black* (1943), *Tin Pan Alley Cats* (1943), *Book Revue* (1945—misspelled "Book Review" in the re-release prints), *Baby Bottle-neck* (1945), *Kitty Kornered* (1946), and *The Great Piggy Bank Robbery* (1946). Clampett was always concerned primarily with the personalities of the characters, but his conceptualizing of his films went far beyond the examples (other than Disney's illustrated music) in the preceding two paragraphs; he conceived his pictures as an almost unrestricted expression of his (and his characters') emotions. "I thought of the movie screen as a sort of magic canvas for my imagination," he once remarked. Clampett would often take long walks along the beach in the evenings, running his latest story visually over and over in his mind until he had a clear idea of every detail of the picture. (Any section that remained unclear was usually the result of an unresolved story point, which he would discuss the next day with his story man.) He allowed his imagination to run riot, thinking only of what he would ideally like to see on some magic movie screen. Only afterwards did he worry about how to achieve those visuals on paper and on the camera stand. Of course, he was instinctively aware of a few

practical considerations—the Warner budgets could not afford detailed crowd scenes or animated backgrounds. Some of his visual ideas had to be modified for various technical reasons, but the important point is that he achieved so much more visual excitement on the screen than anyone would have in their more literal-minded thinking because he dared to consider more imaginative possibilities. For example, in some of his cartoons the backgrounds (the characters' environments) change color or become distorted, mid scene, as the "emotional environment" is affected by the characters' intense feelings. In *Book Revue* the background doesn't change color—the intensity of the color (the intensity of Daffy Duck's emotions) obliterates the background: the whole screen (except for Daffy himself), mid scene, turns solid red. Sometimes the characters themselves become distorted into different sizes, shapes and colors, as reflections of their intense emotions.

An important point that should be kept in mind, for the purpose of our discussion here, is that none of these things happened for the sake of a gag, or a visual pun, as does happen in some other directors' cartoons (most notably Tex Avery's, in his 1940s M.G.M.cartoons). Also, similar character-motivated visual "intensities" do sometimes occur in Disney's earlier feature length cartoons but, with a few exceptions, they are so restrained that they usually lack the punch that a bolder version could have had. The point I am making here is that a highly subjective, impressionistic use of colors and

*Recommended books for the study of film direction.*

shapes, to express the emotions of the central characters, combined with visual ideas derived from expressionist art and theater stage design, could lend themselves to the telling of stories intelligent and adult enough to win the public's admiration and respect.

Another very important part of a successful director's job is to emotionally and artistically inspire all the people working on the film, so that they fully understand the director's personal artistic vision and want to help to make the best possible film. This alone accomplishes something that no amount of money can buy. To do this, of course, a director has to have a very clear vision of his artistic goal, and yet be alert to good suggestions (when they appear) from the crew. The crew members are the director's primary tools, for better or worse, and so the wise director will realistically consider the strengths as well as the limitations of his individual crew members.

It is difficult to recommend specific books on film direction because direction is such an all-embracing subject—and there is a continual flow of new books every year on subjects related to film direction. There are books in which live action directors discuss their work, but mostly there are books on the individual phases of a director's job. For example: stage lighting and the psychological and emotional effects of that; cutting, editing, film scoring (composing music for film), and camera equipment and lenses (which is applicable to shooting on a multiplane animation stand). One book I might mention (in addition to the ones already listed in the earlier chapters) is *Grammar of the Film Language* by Daniel Arijon, 1976, Focal Press, $65.00 (624 pages, with

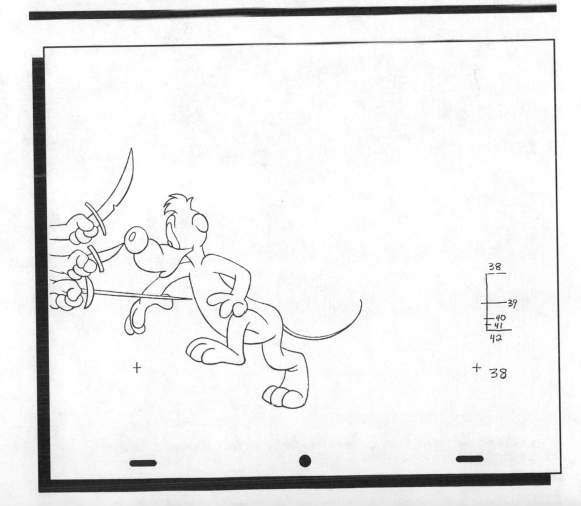

*Disney's **The Martins and the Coys,** a segment from the feature **Make Mine Music** (1946).*
©Walt Disney Productions

lots of illustrations, hardback), which, among other things, probably covers about every different kind of continuity-cutting problem that a director could encounter. Film cutting may not appear to be difficult until one encounters a two- (or more) character sequence that seems to absolutely require violating the basic principles of "screen direction" (meaning: characters moving toward screen left or screen right), thereby creating unwanted audience confusion; this book offers several solutions to those kinds of problems. Another book of particular interest to animation directors, since cartoon films must be edited and timed right down to individual frames prior to actual animation production, is *On Film Editing* by Edward Dmytryk, 1984, Focal Press, $10.95 (paperback) which explains clearly the practice and theories of film editing for the best artistic effect, from the point of view of a man who is both a film editor and a live action film director. Other than that, I would suggest that you check your local library, or contact Larry Edmunds' Bookshop for current recommendations (mailing address listed near the end of chapter five). Two live action film magazines, which occasionally contain valuable articles on directing, writing and producing, are *American Film,* P.O. Box 2046, Marion, Ohio 43306-2146, and *Film Comment,* P.O. Box 3000, Denville, NJ 07834-9924. Write to them for their subscription rates.

An anticipated book on American animation history, with special emphasis on analyzing animation's past achievements in a manner that will give valuable insight to tomorrow's cartoon film makers, is being written by Michael Barrier. This book will

*Casey and his teammates in Disney's*
**Casey at the Bat**, *from the feature*
**Make Mine Music** *(1946).*
©Walt Disney Productions

cover all of the old Hollywood theatrical cartoon studios, and will be published by Oxford University Press.

Three animation books that give some insight into the nuts-and-bolts side of cartoon film production, at least on the film school level, are: *The Animation Book* by Kit Laybourne, 1979, Crown Publishers, $14.95 (paperback), and two books in the Kodak film manual series, *The World of Animation* (1979; $7.95), and *The Complete Kodak Animation Book* (1983; $17.95). The Kodak film manual series is sold in many camera supply stores.

By now it must be apparent that theatrical animation, like the larger live action film industry, is both an entertainment and a mass-communication business. Your job is to communicate to the world everything that you know about life—otherwise, more interesting entertainers will attract the audiences. My best personal advice to anyone still in high school, or earlier, is get a head start—start learning as many different things as you can now. Once you leave high school, you will probably never again have the opportunity to get a free education.

*Disney's **All the Cats Join In**, from the feature **Make Mine Music**.* ©Walt Disney Productions

# VII.  THE ANIMATION FILM PRODUCER

The ideal animation producer is someone who understands the art of animation well enough to recognize what is needed artistically and whom to hire as writers, directors, designers, and the heads of departments in layout, animation, and ink and paint. Furthermore, such a producer must have a good business head to deal with film distributors, bankers, tax boards, accountants, unions, attorneys, public relations, national advertising campaigns, and a host of other details. And he must find a way to acquire several million dollars to invest in a feature length animated film (since there is not yet an established market outlet to pay for quality short subjects).

Animation has long been considered a prohibitively expensive medium, but in truth its costs compare favorably with those of live action—at least if it is placed in the proper hands. Animated films have acquired a reputation for failure at the theater boxoffice, yet a few do occasionally get financed. Since 1960 over thirty non-Disney American-made theatrical feature length cartoons have been financed and produced, and all but four of them have died in the theaters. Of course, one look at the films themselves explains why they died, but that's an artistic judgement and financial investors tend to look only at the ledgers.

Some of those feature length cartoons were financed for strange reasons, and were probably not intended for much more than a quick playoff in Saturday matinees

before being rushed to television. But financing and marketing an artistically success-ful feature cartoon requires careful planning and entails a degree of financial risk for an aspiring producer with limited financial means and no unusual business connections.

The next few paragraphs will outline one possible route for acquiring financing for a feature length theatrical cartoon (we will assume that producing a feature length theatrical cartoon is the best way to secure the largest budget per screen minute, to maintain the most artistic freedom, and to score the most conspicuous box office success):

The producer's first step will be the most crucial: selecting a promising property to develop, or a writer with a good story idea. A writer must be selected with great care and caution. Many writers, like so many of anything else, are hacks and incompetents and do not deserve to be put on pedestals. But the relative few good ones are gold.

The second step will involve the largest part of the producer's financial risk: to have the story developed in storyboard form, and to have the storyboard shot on film as a series of still drawings, timed to the general length of the scenes, with a dummy sound track to approximate the dialog. (This will henceforth be referred to as the "story reel.") (It is possible, if one has the right business connections and a lot of luck, to sell a feature cartoon with only a verbal pitch and a few pieces of artwork, but success from taking that route is extremely unlikely for an "unproven" producer, and it invites artistic interference by the financier.)

There are a number of good reasons for making a complete story reel. One is to be certain in one's own mind that the story is working—visually as well as in plot struc-ture. Another is to be able to give a very clear idea to prospective financial backers of what the story is, who the characters are and how well they will "read" on film, and generally how the film itself will look and how well the story will "play" on the screen.

If time and money permit, it would also be highly advisable to fully animate, in color, the first minute or two of the film, to give a more complete idea of how the finished film would look. Otherwise, people are likely to read into your unfinished work the most incompetent animation they have seen elsewhere, because bad animation is so prevalent (especially on TV), and because they may have unspoken doubts about your actual ability to produce a high quality product. A lot of people with seemingly excellent credentials have acquired financial backing, only to produce very badly animated films. Even to professional live action filmmakers, animation is a largely unknown—and therefore unquantifiable—technique; consequently they are quite leery of it.

The next five minutes of your story reel, ideally, ought to be very well directed pencil drawings of the key poses of the characters—almost the animation extremes without the completed animation. (When this is done for an entire film, or an entire sequence, it is called a "pose reel.") This gives a more complete feeling of the proposed personality acting of the characters than could be gotten from only storyboard sketches, and it makes an appropriate transition from the first minute or so of finished animation to the remaining eighty or so minutes of your story reel.

The most likely financial backers to approach are the heads of the major film distribution companies—Warners, Paramount, 20th Century Fox, etc. (The heads of these companies will henceforth be referred to as "the majors.") Trying to sell a film story to the majors is a good test of the story itself, because if it won't sell to the majors, chances are it wouldn't sell to the public either.

If the story you are trying to sell is as good as it should be, the chances of attracting the interest of one or more of the majors is pretty decent. Good (salable) film stories are hard to find, and the distribution companies are in fierce competition with each other for the few good stories that come along, because each of these companies has to distribute at least six or eight theatrical features a year to amortize their overhead. The major film companies, of course, make most of the films that they distribute, but it is common for an independent producer to get financial backing from a major company if he owns a sufficiently promising story and if he insists on producing it himself. In the jargon of the industry, that is called "blackmail."

Stories are normally submitted to the major studios in the form of typewritten scripts (mostly for live action films) from writers, agents and producers. The number of such scripts that each major studio receives each week is staggering, and the percentage of those scripts that are unusable is also staggering. Each of the major studios employs full-time "readers" to plow through this sea of paper. If a script doesn't look promising to a reader after the first few pages, it will not be read further. Occasionally, if so many scripts have been submitted that the readers can't get to them all in a few week's time, some may be returned unopened. The majors want to know about the few good stories that get written, and the trick is, if you have such a story how do you make yourself "visible" in that sea of submissions? The majors themselves, in seminars with filmmakers and aspiring filmmakers, have stated a possible solution: If you have a genuinely good story, show it around, to anyone in the business who will look at it—

presumably after you've either copyrighted it or at least registered it with the Writers Guild*. If it is genuinely good, those people will talk about it and word will travel up the grapevine to the majors, and they will come to you requesting to see your story. In these seminars, most of the majors claimed to have located (and financed) some of their biggest hits through word-of-mouth.

Always accompany a story reel to any screening. Do not just send the film around or sharks will grab it and take it around, claiming to be your representative and making fancy deals for themselves.

Most majors, when looking at an independent's film, hope that the film (the story) will interest them in the first thirty seconds. If it doesn't do so within the first three minutes, they will not look at the rest. The first thirty seconds are particularly important because of the need to grab the attention of the theater audience.

As soon as a major responds favorably to your story reel, you will have to be prepared to talk business. The major will probably propose—or be the most receptive to—a "step deal," and will want to see a prepared "cost breakdown" of your proposed film project. A step deal allows the major to see your film at each major phase, or "step," of production before he advances to you the financing for the next step. Cartoon film making is perfectly suited for a step deal, which is advantageous to both the major and the producer.

The advantage of the step deal to the producer is that he can use it to buy time. Because of tax schedules, interest rates and ledger sheets, once the majors lay out an investment of several million dollars in a film, they want that film finished and "in the can" in less than a year. Most live action films can accomplish that easily. Animation films, to be made properly, require much more production time; however, the stages of production prior to animation involve a relatively small staff, necessitating an outlay of money small enough to be considered inconsequential to a major film company.

The producer should be careful to include in writing, in any contractual negotiations with the majors, a firm understanding that the film being produced—at each "step," and in its final form—must be identical to the story reel in story, staging, dialog, and the look of the characters, and that neither the producer nor the major can make any significant changes without the written consent of the other, specifying those changes. The selling point to the majors is that this assures them of getting the film they paid for. The advantage to the producer is that this protects him from arbitrary cuts or changes by the major, at any time during or after production. This is another advantage of having a story reel.

The first step of a step deal—the point of completion which the producer presents to the major—would be the "production board." Presumably, the initial story board which was shot on the story reel simply told the story and defined the characters' personalities, with not a lot of visual detail worked out beyond that. The "production board" is a revised storyboard that defines more precisely each scene in the film,

---

* Writers Guild of America, West, Inc., 8955 Beverly Boulevard, Los Angeles, California 90048. Telephone (213) 550-1000. Registration fee is $10.00 for 5 years to non-members, plus one typewritten photocopy on 8 $\frac{1}{2}$" x 11" paper. Registrations are renewable.

indicates every cut and dissolve and the basic camera moves such as the trucks and pans, and includes fairly detailed sketches of all the key locations. This is the preliminary stage of direction. The steps of production to be undertaken during the production board period would vary according to the type of story involved, but would include most of the following:

(1) Atmosphere and mood sketches

(2) Design of locale

(3) Experimental color sketches (color that is subjective rather than literal)

(4) Character design (preliminary model sheets—general appearance plus stretch and squash potential)

(5) Decisions on scene cuts, camera angles

(6) Research for props, costumes, vehicles, locations (both clippings and new photography)

(7) Research for how to do needed unusual special effects

(8) Researching and compiling film clips (live action and animation) for necessary dances, eccentric walks, effects

(9) Auditioning voice people and cataloging the names and tapes

(10) Selecting styles of music (from records)

(11) Selecting (generally) imaginative sound effects

(12) Selecting composers and sound effects people

(13) Hiring a song writer

(14) Selecting necessary layout artists and background painters for the style of backgrounds

(15) Typing scripts for the voice actors

The second step of the step deal—assuming the major approves the production board—would be the "pose reel." This is actually the period during which the film will be directed; everything will be completed prior to actual animation production. The steps of production to be undertaken during the pose reel period would include:

(1) Hire voice actors and book time reservations in recording studios; record voices

(2) Read dialog tracks

(3) Hire a composer

(4) Locate studio space

(5) Buy art supplies for entire film: paper, pencils, desks and discs, cels, paints, brushes, folders, exposure sheets, etc. (Supplies should be ordered early to insure against unexpected shortages)

(6) Install an office photocopy machine and an animation photocopy machine

(7) Background and character layouts—thinking film direction and animation direction in detail

(8) Final model sheets

(9) Character color models

(10) Color key scenes

(11) Final timing of scenes and timing ex-sheets

(12) Some experimental animation of the main characters

(13) Shoot pose reel (on 35mm)

The final step of the step deal is the finished film. Animation, inbetweening, and ink and paint are by far the most expensive stages in cartoon production. They involve the largest numbers of people, but the work flow overlaps significantly so that most of it can be done almost simultaneously. With the film and the animation action already directed and timed, the director can concentrate on directing the animators and guiding them through difficult scenes. With the bulk of the experimenting and planning done in the previous two "steps," the film should now go through final production in less than a year with a minimum of snags. The steps of production to be undertaken during the final period would include:

(1) Animation

(2) Inbetweening

(3) Pencil test

(4) Checking

(5) Background painting

(6) Photocopy/inking; photocopy checking

(7) Cel painting

(8) Final checking

(9) Cel cleaning

(10) Camera

(11) Record music

(12) Record sound effects

(13) Cutting dailies

(14) Shoot titles and credits
(15) Dubbing
(16) Final editing
(17) Cut negative
(18) First answer print
(19) Color correct negative
(20) Final answer print

    The cost breakdown, which the majors will want to see before talking serious business, will require careful planning. The producer dares not overlook any expenses before committing himself to a price, and he will likely be asked to account for every dollar listed. Therefore, prior to figuring a cost breakdown, the producer should acquaint himself with:

 (1) All the labs, services and suppliers, to know the people, the reliability of the products, and the prices.
 (2) The wage scales and contract terms of the unions and guilds representing the musicians, cameramen, editors, directors, animators, voices, bookkeepers and secretaries.
 (3) Attorneys (for writing and reading contract proposals), guarantors, buildings and landlords (for studio space), to learn the costs and terms for each.

The producer will also have to estimate the number of weeks of work that will be needed, in each talent category, times salaries (in the calendar year that the work will be done, since union wage scales escalate each year), union fees (retirement, motion picture health and welfare) and government fees (workmen's compensation, social security). He should include a "producer's fee" to cover the cost of story development for a second feature, and the cost of a color separation preservation negative to protect against color fading and the major distributor's damage or "misplacement" of the original negative. And he should include a ten percent contingency, built into each cost category, to cover errors and retakes. "Errors and retakes" actually covers a multitude of problems, including talent quitting, talent not performing, camera errors just as you are pushing a deadline (which means retakes on overtime), people forgetting to deliver artwork or sound transfers, artwork and tapes getting lost or damaged, labs ruining prints or negatives, or (heaven forbid) the possibility that the finished film, seen as a whole for the first time, turns out much more violent (or whatever) than originally intended.

Studio overhead, for cost breakdown figuring, might include but not be limited to the following:

Supplies and equipment:

(1) art supplies (paper, pencils, tape, cels, paints, brushes, folders, exposure sheets, etc.);
(2) animation desks and discs;
(3) office desks and drawing boards;
(4) checkers' tables and planning bars;
(5) chairs, lamps, overhead lighting, light bulbs and tubes;
(6) pencil sharpeners and waste paper baskets;
(7) cassette recorders, tapes, ear phones;
(8) shelving and drying racks;
(9) paper punch;
(10) airbrush equipment;
(11) filing cabinets;
(12) locks;
(13) hand tools;
(14) building repair and equipment repair;
(15) toilet supplies and paper towels;
(16) first aid supplies;
(17) fire extinguishers and fireproofing;
(18) office photocopy machine;
(19) animation photocopy machine;
(20) daily time cards;
(21) scene folders, exposure sheets, bar sheets, field charts and field guides (12- and 16- field);
(22) typewriters, adding machines, calculators, typing paper, envelopes, stamps or postage meter;
(23) coffee, sugar, cream, coffee machine, bottled water, water cooler, small refrigerator;
(24) concession dispensor machines (soft drinks, snacks, candy, cigarets);

(25) art books and reference books;

(26) videotape or video disc player;

(27) tape or disc rentals for reference and study;

(28) 35mm still camera, tape deck;

(29) Movieola, editing equipment, empty reels, splicer;

(30) three or four video pencil test machines for the animators;

(31) pressboard for walls, for pinning up storyboards and other production artwork.

Services, fees, and taxes:

(1) attorney fees (for financing contracts, talent contracts, distribution contracts, advertising and promotion contracts, service contracts, building lease contracts, etc.);

(2) guarantor's fee or percentages;

(3) business licences and permits;

(4) business taxes (Federal, State, County and City);

(5) rent or lease of studio building;

(6) parking spaces;

(7) janitorial services;

(8) refuse pick-up;

(9) security guard;

(10) electricity, water, gas;

(11) telephones (for producer, director, production manager, secretary, receptionist, bookkeeper, accountant, editor, heads of departments, and a pay phone);
(12) air conditioning and heating;
(13) producer's fee;
(14) business employees (bookkeeper, accountant, secretary, receptionist, production manager, "go-pher");
(15) motor transportation for gopher;
(16) state unemployment insurance, state workmen's disability and social security;
(17) employee severance pay, holiday pay, vacation pay, sick pay;
(18) union pension plan, motion picture health and welfare;
(19) insurance on building, equipment, product (film production), and personnel;
(20) research services and use fees (copyright clearances, sound effects libraries and music libraries);
(21) publicity photos of studio, staff, and work in production;
(22) large photos of storyboards for director, layout artists, animators;
(23) lab services (titling, film processing, recording, mixing, and printing);
(24) sound recording studios and dubbing studios;
(25) screening room rentals;
(26) loan interest;
(27) Motion Picture Ratings Board;
(28) copyright (registration fee plus two release prints).

For tax and bookkeeping reasons the majors often set up, on paper, separate companies to "finance" each new independent feature. Make sure you are a member of the board of any company set up to handle your film, so that you have at least one vote on what that company tries to do with—and to—your film.

On average, cartoon features have been far more difficult to sell than live action features, primarily because of the overwhelming number of non-Disney cartoon features that have been badly made—and have consequently been commercial flops—in the past three decades.

Recently there has been a resurgence of financing and production of cartoon theatrical features in Los Angeles, and if these features are well written and well made—and then promoted and marketed properly—so that they become commercial successes at the boxoffice, they could ease the resistance against cartoon features. Otherwise, things will become as difficult as before.

The people running the major Hollywood film distribution companies—the decision makers—do not own the companies; consequently they are expendable and easily replaced, and are typically made the scapegoats whenever the company has films in release that do not perform well at the boxoffice. Therefore the decision makers invariably try to protect themselves by giving the green light to only those film projects that contain elements which were successful ("bankable") in the past: well-known stars, directors, writers and certain story themes. These elements are "insurance"— they provide "proof" that the decision makers exercised reasonable judgement when giving the green light to a project which subsequently failed to be as commercially successful as expected.

Cartoon features, especially considering the bad reputation they have acquired over the past three decades, have little to offer. Even using famous movie stars as voices of the characters is a pretty poor attempt at including "bankable elements." Worse, the movie theater owners dislike cartoon features because cartoons traditionally have not performed well, and to the extent that they do perform, they typically attract children, whose tickets sell for less money. Consequently, the distributors' sales people dislike cartoons because they are forced to deal with the resistance of the theater owners.

Furthermore, a new producer is at a disadvantage against the large established cartoon studios because of those studios' "proven track record," plus the fact that they have already in place all the necessary equipment, working space and trained staff, plus the probability that they have enough financial resources to guarantee the completion of a film if it goes over budget (which makes it easier to be accepted by a guarantor). Plus, the established studios typically have ongoing subcontracting relationships with studios in foreign countries, which is helpful if the producer needs to save money on part of the production, such as cel painting.

For the above reasons, the major Hollywood film distribution companies may delay almost indefinitely giving a new producer the green light. Obviously a tremendous burden is being placed on the quality of that producer's story and its presentation, since that alone must outweigh all the negatives.

Fortunately, in recent years several of the biggest boxoffice successes in live action have been essentially "comic book movies": *Batman, Superman, Dick Tracy,*

*Ghostbusters,* plus the Indiana Jones and Star Wars trilogies. Also, if the individual decision makers at the major distribution companies seem disposed against giving a cartoon the green light, it may be only a matter of time before those individuals are replaced. At most of the majors, the average tenure of the top people has been about two to three years.

Another alternative is to seek outside financing for your project from private investors. This greatly increases the number of potential sources of financing, but it also requires extraordinary salesmanship. Plus, for every person who does invest, you will have to court, individually, a hundred pretenders who only want to tell their friends how they had a dinner meeting (at your expense) with "a movie producer." This is a route often taken by independent producers, and it helps enormously in securing a film distribution deal with a major. A major will give a far better deal to the investor, since the financial risk is shared (plus you have the psychological advantage of demonstrating that someone else has faith in your project).

Cartoons have yet another disadvantage compared with live action: the absence of glamour. Regardless of the source of financing, whether from private investors or a major distribution company, with live action films the fear of financial risk is offset by the allure of rubbing elbows with famous directors, charismatic movie stars, sexy starlets. Such adventures may be the thrill of a lifetime for the average investor. Animation, by contrast, consists only of a roomful of artists hunched over drawing

*Books recommended as preparation for becoming a film producer.*

boards like so many accountants; the magic is all in their heads (and, hopefully, in the final product).

In the current era of home video, animation that is well produced is considered a safer investment, since animation titles on videotape are far more likely to be purchased than rented, on the expectation that children will want to watch them over and over. Animation titles, both Disney and non-Disney, tend to dominate Variety's lists of the top ten videotape sellers. As Walt Disney has stated, good cartoon action "will keep the children constantly amused, even if the subject occasionally goes over their heads." (Quoted in the book *Walt Disney's World of Fantasy*, by Adrian Bailey, 1982, page 116.)

Relatively new animation producers have been building track records, first by performing well on low budget local TV commercials, and animation inserts into industrial and educational films, and in time graduating to high budget national TV commercials, animation inserts into TV shows and live action features, and finally producing TV specials or series on the growing cable TV networks.

At least one animator-director, years ago, travelled a route similar to that in the book *The Movie Brats* by Michael Pye and Linda Myles, 1979, Holt, Rinehart and Winston, $14.95 (paperback), which describes how the most successful new live action theatrical film producer-directors worked their way from the bottom to the top of the industry. Basically, they each got their first break by directing super-low budget features, usually horror movies for drive-ins, costing under one-half million dollars (in

the early 1970s) for exploitation film distributors. By any conventional standard, it is impossible to turn out a feature length cartoon for a price that low. But in 1973, Charles Swenson directed and single-handedly animated, in one year, a feature length cartoon, *Dirty Duck,* reportedly for $100,000. I couldn't believe it until I saw it; the cartoon was not animated in any classical sense, but consisted instead of very crude but fully moving drawings of very simple characters—characters that were scarcely more than doodles, but nevertheless wryly appealing. Swenson reportedly animated very quickly, directly onto cels with a grease pencil. (The cels and backgrounds were painted by other people.) The film is seriously flawed by the lack of a coherent story, but it does have inspired moments, when Swenson matched very expressive renditions of his characters with equally expressive voices (which sound like imaginative voice people ad-libbing). These moments clearly indicate how good a low budget film such as this could have been. (*Dirty Duck* has been released on videotape.)

For any film, whether made on a low or high budget, to survive in the major theatrical film market, the minimum necessary expense for advertising, promotion and distribution would be several million dollars. This means that, ironically, financing a low budget picture may require a greater leap of faith than financing a more expensive film; the backer must have tremendous confidence that the filmmakers can turn out a winning film on a shoestring.

Making big money as a film maker is a long range proposition. Established, successful film makers (meaning, film makers whose features have made big money at the box office) can demand from the majors a percentage (called percentage "points") of the "profits." Aspiring, unproven film makers are lucky just to have their proposed projects financed, and to receive a salary during production. "Profits" is a suspect word in the movie business. It is defined as the monies remaining after the distributor's expenses and the "distributor's fee" have been subtracted from the "gross"—the rental fees paid to the distributor by the movie theaters. The "distributor's fee" is the real bone of contention. It is always contractually specified as a certain percentage of the gross, usually somewhere between thirty and forty percent, and has nothing to do with covering distribution expenses. Many film makers regard it as legalized robbery, but it serves a legitimate purpose: The majors have to finance the "negative cost" (the cost of production) of all—or nearly all—of the films they distribute, and not all of those films attract enough of an audience to make money past their negative cost and actual distribution expenses (which include the cost of prints of the film and the advertising, as well as the correspondence, collecting, bookkeeping and shipping). No one can tell for sure, in advance, which films will be the hits, but the "distributor's fee" is the major's way of covering their losses with monies from the hits. Once a film maker has made one or two substantially successful films, he or she is in a position to bargain ("blackmail") the majors into giving a number of points on subsequent films.

In most business and legal respects, producing cartoon films is the same as producing live action films. There are a number of books available on film producing, including: *The Film Industries* by Michael F. Mayer, 1973, 1978, Hastings House, $13.00, and *Independent Feature Film Production* by Gregory Goodell, 1982, St. Martin, $11.95 (paperback). Such books are must reading for an aspiring producer. They explain things to look out for in contracts with financiers and distributors, clearing rights to music, literary and other copyrighted sources, laws that relate to film content versus privacy and defamation, how to protect created characters and sequels, theatrical and non-theatrical markets, and a multitude of other film business and legal problems.

Since any filmmaking business (including animation) necessitates being a part of the larger Hollywood film industry, and being enormously affected by the business politics of that industry, a recent book of excellent investigative reporting deserves a special mention: *Reel Power* by Mark Litwak, 1986, Plume, $9.95 (paperback). The power structure of Hollywood is very different than the layman would expect, and a great many regrettable business decisions get made due to complex patterns of business political pressures on the decision-makers. This book makes the seemingly insane business decisions understandable, and therefore easier to anticipate and deal with.

On the darker side, bear in mind that any business or industry that handles hundreds of millions of dollars in short periods of time is going to attract an endless array of crooks, cheats, liars, and greed and corruption of all kinds. This seems particularly true of the so-called "glamour" industries. Responsible newspapers and magazines, including The Los Angeles Times and TV Guide, have carried a great many feature articles of investigation into alleged charges, against several of the majors, of

fraud and unethical practices. One good article, for example, is "How Hollywood Studios Flimflam Their Stars," which appeared in the May 1, 1982, issue of TV Guide (to see that issue, check your library). One of the warnings to emerge from these articles is that it would appear to be unwise to rent space or equipment from the majors, even though they may urge you to do so, because their charges may well be outrageous. And on any contract they present that promises profit participation points on your film, be more than suspicious of any "fees" and "charges" that they allow themselves (the amount of which they will identify at a later date); this appears to be an issue that goes far beyond the "legitimate purpose" mentioned earlier regarding the standard percentage "distributor's fee." At least one good book on this subject is *Indecent Exposure* by David McClintick, 1982, Dell, $3.95 (paperback). While it will do no good to walk into any business negotiation with a chip on one's shoulder, it is well to be knowledgeable about the whole spectrum of the business one is dealing with.

The market for film product is changing rapidly, as outlined in chapter one, and the continuing growth of home video, both domestic and foreign, represents the most encouraging marketplace for cartoons, features and shorts alike. Old traditions of marketing cartoons are only beginning to yield to the new realities of the marketplace. Despite the current pitfalls identified in this chapter, the opportunities are growing and the rewards will be enormous for those who make a concerted effort and learn the art of cartoon filmmaking well enough to do it right.

# APPENDIX

### Union Wage Minimums (1990-1993)

On the following pages are the minimum wage scales for all categories of artists and technicians in the Los Angeles Motion Picture Screen Cartoonists Union, computed into dollars per hour and per week. It should be noted that in addition to the minimum wage scales, the union also guarantees all union employees holiday pay, vacation pay, payment towards the employee's retirement pension, severance pay (when appropriate), and automatic paid membership in a very complete group health insurance package.

Most Los Angeles animation studios are signatories to the union contract. This means that if you change jobs, from one studio to another, your health insurance and other benefits will continue.

The categories in which the largest number of new people will be hired are listed on page 102. Beginners in the animation department are called inbetweeners, who subsequently graduate to breakdown and then to assistant animators. Beginners in layout and storyboard (job descriptions on page 24) are called apprentice layout and apprentice production board people (listed near the bottom of page 102). (Layout and storyboard people do not go through the "breakdown" category as they graduate upward; "breakdown" applies only to the animation department.)

MOTION PICTURE SCREEN CARTOONISTS, LOCAL 839 I. A. T. S. E.
Wage Scales, August 1, 1990—July 31, 1993
Weekly employment*

| CODE | CLASSIFICATION | First year 8/1/90 —7/31/91 | | Second year 8/1/91—7/31/92 | | Third year 8/1/92—7/31/93 | |
|------|----------------|--------|--------|--------|--------|--------|--------|
| | | HOURLY | WEEKLY | HOURLY | WEEKLY | HOURLY | WEEKLY |
| ANIMATION | | | | | | | |
| 21-012 | Animator** | | | | | | |
| -032 | Background** | | | | | | |
| -042 | Layout** | | | | | | |
| -052 | Model Designer** | | | | | | |
| -022 | Animation Story Person** | | | | | | |
| | Production Board*** | | | | | | |
| -801 | Staff Comic Strip Story Person and/or Artist | | | | | | |
| | 1st 6 months | $22.020 | $880.80 | $22.901 | $916.04 | $23.817 | $952.68 |
| | 2nd 6 months | 22.541 | 901.64 | 23.443 | 937.72 | 24.381 | 975.24 |
| | Journeyman | 23.415 | 936.60 | 24.352 | 974.08 | 25.326 | 1,013.04 |

(Subject to right of Producer to request extension—limited to one six-month extension)

| | | | | | | | |
|------|----------------|--------|--------|--------|--------|--------|--------|
| 21-112 | Key Assistant Animator | | | | | | |
| | | 22.403 | 896.12 | 23.299 | 931.96 | 24.231 | 969.24 |
| 21-102 | Assistant Animator | | | | | | |
| 21-122 | Assistant Background | | | | | | |
| | Assistant Layout | | | | | | |
| 21-132 | Assistant Model Designer | | | | | | |
| 21-802 | Assistant Staff Comic Strip Story Person and/or Artist | | | | | | |
| | 1st 6 months | 18.521 | 740.84 | 19.262 | 770.48 | 20.032 | 801.28 |
| | 2nd 6 months | 19.002 | 760.08 | 19.762 | 790.48 | 20.552 | 822.08 |
| | Journeyman | 19.913 | 796.52 | 20.710 | 828.40 | 21.538 | 861.52 |

(Subject to right of Producer to request extension—limited to one six-month extension)

| | | | | | | | |
|------|----------------|--------|--------|--------|--------|--------|--------|
| 21-142 | Breakdown | | | | | | |
| | 1st year | 16.897 | 675.88 | 17.573 | 702.92 | 18.276 | 731.04 |
| | Journeyman | 17.389 | 695.56 | 18.085 | 723.40 | 18.808 | 752.32 |
| 21-152 | Inbetweener | | | | | | |
| | 1st 6 months | 15.608 | 624.32 | 16.232 | 649.28 | 16.881 | 675.24 |
| | 2nd 6 months | 16.084 | 643.36 | 16.727 | 669.08 | 17.396 | 695.84 |
| | Journeyman | 16.703 | 668.12 | 17.371 | 694.84 | 18.066 | 722.64 |
| 21-202 | Apprentice Layout, Model Designer, Background and Production Board | | | | | | |
| | 6 months | 16.879 | 675.16 | 17.554 | 702.16 | 18.256 | 730.24 |

(Subject to right of Producer to request one six-month extension)

* Minimum scale for daily employees shall be 117.719% (which rate is inclusive of vacation and holiday pay) of the minimum basic hourly rate provided herein for such employee's classification.
** An Animator, Background or Layout person designated by the Producer to be responsible for and supervise the work of others in his classification shall be paid the key rate of 15% above the minimum Journeyman rate for his classification during such an assignment.
*** Producer agrees to pay to the Production Board classification the key rate of 15% above minimum at all times as provided.

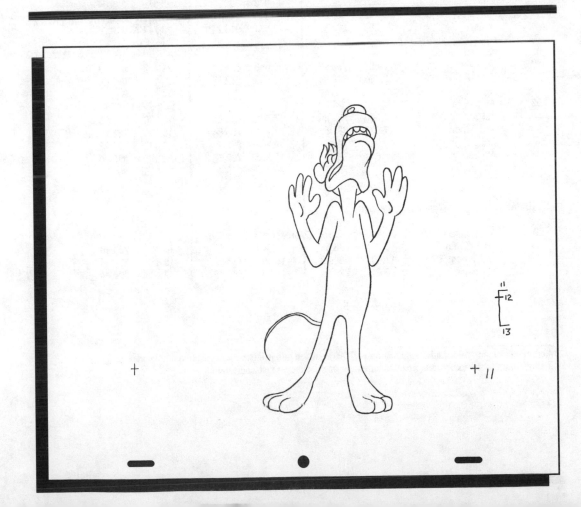

MOTION PICTURE SCREEN CARTOONISTS, LOCAL 839 I. A. T. S. E.
Wage Scales, August 1, 1990—July 31, 1993
Weekly employment*

| CODE | CLASSIFICATION | First year 8/1/90 —7/31/91 HOURLY | WEEKLY | Second year 8/1/91—7/31/92 HOURLY | WEEKLY | Third year 8/1/92—7/31/93 HOURLY | WEEKLY |
|---|---|---|---|---|---|---|---|
| 21-232 | Blue Sketch | | | | | | |
| | First year | $16.540 | $661.60 | $17.202 | $688.08 | $17.890 | $715.60 |
| | Journeyman | 17.039 | 681.56 | 17.721 | 708.84 | 18.430 | 737.20 |
| 21-312 | Story Sketch | | | | | | |
| | First year | 20.625 | 825.00 | 21.450 | 858.00 | 22.308 | 892.32 |
| | Journeyman | 20.955 | 838.20 | 21.793 | 871.72 | 22.665 | 906.60 |
| 21-322 | Apprentice Animation Story Person and/or Apprentice Story Sketch | | | | | | |
| | 1st 6 months | 16.924 | 676.96 | 17.601 | 704.04 | 18.305 | 732.20 |
| | 2nd 6 months | 19.611 | 784.44 | 20.395 | 815.80 | 21.211 | 848.44 |
| | (Subject to right of Producer to request extension—limited to one six-month extension) | | | | | | |
| 21-332 | Assistant Director | | | | | | |
| | 1st 6 months | 17.623 | 704.92 | 18.328 | 733.12 | 19.061 | 762.44 |
| | 2nd 6 months | 19.301 | 772.04 | 20.073 | 802.92 | 20.876 | 835.04 |
| | 3rd 6 months | 20.980 | 839.20 | 21.819 | 872.76 | 22.692 | 907.68 |
| | Journeyman | 21.953 | 878.12 | 22.831 | 913.24 | 23.744 | 949.76 |
| 21-335 | Sheet Timer | | | | | | |
| | 1st 6 months | 17.623 | 704.92 | 18.328 | 733.12 | 19.061 | 762.44 |
| | 2nd 6 months | 19.301 | 772.04 | 20.073 | 802.92 | 20.876 | 835.04 |
| | 3rd 6 months | 20.980 | 839.20 | 21.819 | 872.76 | 22.692 | 907.68 |
| | Journeyman | 21.953 | 878.12 | 22.831 | 913.24 | 23.744 | 949.76 |
| 21-242 | Scene Planner | | | | | | |
| | First year | 19.862 | 794.48 | 20.656 | 826.24 | 21.482 | 859.28 |
| | Journeyman | 20.721 | 828.84 | 21.550 | 862.00 | 22.412 | 896.48 |
| 21-252 | Animation Checker | | | | | | |
| | 1st 3 months | 16.540 | 661.60 | 17.202 | 688.08 | 17.890 | 715.60 |
| | 2nd 9 months | 17.039 | 681.56 | 17.721 | 708.84 | 18.430 | 737.20 |
| | 3rd 6 months | 18.521 | 740.84 | 19.262 | 770.48 | 20.032 | 801.28 |
| | 4th 6 months | 19.041 | 761.64 | 19.803 | 792.12 | 20.595 | 823.80 |
| | Journeyman | 19.913 | 796.52 | 20.710 | 828.40 | 21.538 | 861.52 |

INK AND PAINT (Inking, Special Effects, Painters)

| CODE | CLASSIFICATION | HOURLY | WEEKLY | HOURLY | WEEKLY | HOURLY | WEEKLY |
|---|---|---|---|---|---|---|---|
| 21-412 | Assistant Supervisor (Ink and Paint, Xerox, Color Model or Paint Lab) | | | | | | |
| | 1st 6 months | 16.964 | 678.56 | 17.643 | 705.72 | 18.349 | 733.96 |
| | 2nd 6 months | 17.402 | 696.08 | 18.098 | 723.92 | 18.822 | 752.88 |
| | Journeyman | 18.016 | 720.64 | 18.737 | 749.48 | 19.486 | 779.44 |

* Minimum scale for daily employees shall be 117.719% (which rate is inclusive of vacation and holiday pay)
of the minimum basic hourly rate provided herein for such employee's classification.

MOTION PICTURE SCREEN CARTOONISTS, LOCAL 839 I. A. T. S. E.
Wage Scales, August 1, 1990—July 31, 1993
Weekly employment*

| CODE | CLASSIFICATION | First year 8/1/90—7/31/91 HOURLY | WEEKLY | Second year 8/1/91—7/31/92 HOURLY | WEEKLY | Third year 8/1/92—7/31/93 HOURLY | WEEKLY |
|---|---|---|---|---|---|---|---|
| 21-422 | Inker | | | | | | |
| | First month | $14.647 | $585.88 | $15.233 | $609.32 | $15.842 | $633.68 |
| | Next 6 months | 15.488 | 619.52 | 16.108 | 644.32 | 16.752 | 670.08 |
| | Next 6 months | 15.937 | 637.48 | 16.574 | 662.96 | 17.237 | 689.48 |
| | Journeyman | 16.526 | 661.04 | 17.187 | 687.48 | 17.874 | 714.96 |
| 21-442 | Ink Checker | | | | | | |
| | First year | 16.795 | 671.80 | 17.467 | 698.68 | 18.166 | 726.64 |
| | Journeyman | 17.118 | 684.72 | 17.803 | 712.12 | 18.515 | 740.60 |
| 21-452 | Special Effects | | | | | | |
| | First year | 16.795 | 671.80 | 17.467 | 698.68 | 18.166 | 726.64 |
| | Journeyman | 17.118 | 684.72 | 17.803 | 712.12 | 18.515 | 740.60 |
| 21-453 | Head Special Effects | | | | | | |
| | | 17.623 | 704.92 | 18.328 | 733.12 | 19.061 | 762.44 |
| 21-500 | Color Modelist | | | | | | |
| | 1st 6 months | 16.112 | 644.48 | 16.756 | 670.24 | 17.426 | 697.04 |
| | 2nd 6 months | 16.563 | 662.52 | 17.226 | 689.04 | 17.915 | 716.60 |
| | Journeyman | 17.208 | 688.32 | 17.896 | 715.84 | 18.612 | 744.48 |
| 21-522 | Painter | | | | | | |
| | First month | 14.647 | 585.88 | 15.233 | 609.32 | 15.842 | 633.68 |
| | Next 6 months | 15.258 | 610.32 | 15.868 | 634.72 | 16.503 | 660.12 |
| | Next 6 months | 15.724 | 628.96 | 16.353 | 654.12 | 17.007 | 680.28 |
| | Journeyman | 16.399 | 655.96 | 17.055 | 682.20 | 17.737 | 709.48 |
| 21-542 | Xerox Processor | | | | | | |
| | First 3 months | 14.647 | 585.88 | 15.233 | 609.32 | 15.842 | 633.68 |
| | Next 12 months | 16.008 | 640.32 | 16.648 | 665.92 | 17.314 | 692.56 |
| | Journeyman | 16.399 | 655.96 | 17.055 | 682.20 | 17.737 | 709.48 |
| 21-552 | Key Xerox Processor | | | | | | |
| | | 16.617 | 664.68 | 17.282 | 691.28 | 17.973 | 718.92 |
| CHECKERS | | | | | | | |
| 21-562 | Xerox Checker | | | | | | |
| | First year | 16.795 | 671.80 | 17.467 | 698.68 | 18.166 | 726.64 |
| | Journeyman | 17.118 | 684.72 | 17.803 | 712.12 | 18.515 | 740.60 |
| 21-572 | Animation Stock Librarian | | | | | | |
| | 1st 6 months | 16.025 | 641.00 | 16.666 | 666.64 | 17.333 | 693.32 |
| | 2nd 6 months | 16.454 | 658.16 | 17.112 | 684.48 | 17.796 | 711.84 |
| | Journeyman | 17.118 | 684.72 | 17.803 | 712.12 | 18.515 | 740.60 |

* Minimum scale for daily employees shall be 117.719% (which rate is inclusive of vacation and holiday pay) of the minimum basic hourly rate provided herein for such employee's classification.

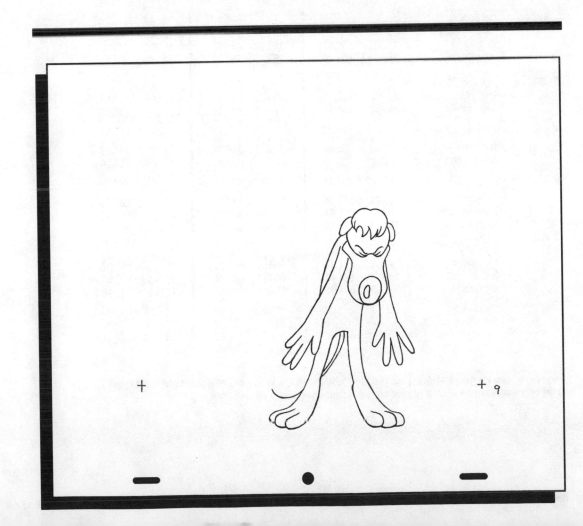

MOTION PICTURE SCREEN CARTOONISTS, LOCAL 839 I. A. T. S. E.
Wage Scales, August 1, 1990—July 31, 1993
Weekly employment*

| CODE | CLASSIFICATION | First year 8/1/90 —7/31/91 | | Second year 8/1/91—7/31/92 | | Third year 8/1/92—7/31/93 | |
|------|----------------|--------|--------|--------|--------|--------|--------|
| | | HOURLY | WEEKLY | HOURLY | WEEKLY | HOURLY | WEEKLY |
| 21-632 | Production Final Checker/Mark-Up | | | | | | |
| | 1st 6 months | $16.025 | $641.00 | $16.666 | $666.64 | $17.333 | $693.32 |
| | 2nd 6 months | 16.454 | 658.16 | 17.112 | 684.48 | 17.796 | 711.84 |
| | Journeyman | 17.118 | 684.72 | 17.803 | 712.12 | 18.515 | 740.60 |
| 21-633 | Head Final Checker | | | | | | |
| | | 17.623 | 704.92 | 18.328 | 733.12 | 19.061 | 762.44 |
| 21-652 | Paint Checker | | | | | | |
| | 1st 6 months | 15.608 | 624.32 | 16.232 | 649.28 | 16.881 | 675.24 |
| | 2nd 6 months | 16.084 | 643.36 | 16.727 | 669.08 | 17.396 | 695.84 |
| | Journeyman | 16.703 | 668.12 | 17.371 | 694.84 | 18.066 | 722.64 |
| 21-672 | Picture Set-Up | | | | | | |
| | First year | 16.540 | 661.60 | 17.202 | 688.08 | 17.890 | 715.60 |
| | Journeyman | 17.093 | 683.72 | 17.777 | 711.08 | 18.488 | 739.52 |
| 21-682 | Scan Checker | | | | | | |
| | 1st 6 months | 15.181 | 607.24 | 15.788 | 631.52 | 16.420 | 656.80 |
| | 2nd 6 months | 15.622 | 624.88 | 16.247 | 649.88 | 16.897 | 675.88 |
| | Journeyman | 16.222 | 648.88 | 16.871 | 674.84 | 17.546 | 701.84 |
| 21-692 | Cel Service | | | | | | |
| | 1st 6 months | 15.105 | 604.20 | 15.709 | 628.36 | 16.337 | 653.48 |
| | 2nd 6 months | 15.521 | 620.84 | 16.142 | 645.68 | 16.788 | 671.52 |
| | Journeyman | 16.044 | 641.76 | 16.686 | 667.44 | 17.353 | 694.12 |
| 21-722 | Mix and Match | | | | | | |
| | First year | 15.803 | 632.12 | 16.435 | 657.40 | 17.092 | 683.68 |
| | Journeyman | 16.463 | 658.52 | 17.122 | 684.88 | 17.807 | 712.28 |
| 21-742 | Paint Technician | | | | | | |
| | First year | 17.134 | 685.36 | 17.819 | 712.76 | 18.532 | 741.28 |
| | Journeyman | 17.760 | 710.40 | 18.470 | 738.80 | 19.209 | 768.36 |
| 21-792 | Letter Artist | | | | | | |
| | 1st 6 months | 18.521 | 740.84 | 19.262 | 770.48 | 20.032 | 801.28 |
| | 2nd 6 months | 19.041 | 761.64 | 19.803 | 792.12 | 20.595 | 823.80 |
| | Journeyman | 19.913 | 796.52 | 20.710 | 828.40 | 21.538 | 861.52 |
| 21-222 | Trainee | | | | | | |
| | 1st 6 months | 14.861 | 594.44 | 15.455 | 618.20 | 16.073 | 642.92 |
| | 2nd 6 months | 15.612 | 624.48 | 16.236 | 649.44 | 16.885 | 675.40 |
| | 3rd 6 months | 16.363 | 654.52 | 17.018 | 680.72 | 17.699 | 707.96 |

* Minimum scale for daily employees shall be 117.719% (which rate is inclusive of vacation and holiday pay) of the minimum basic hourly rate provided herein for such employee's classification.

# BIBLIOGRAPHY

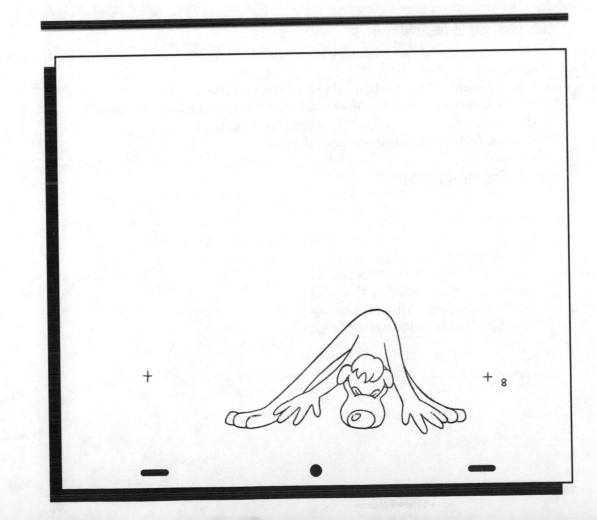

The following books are described in some detail on various pages throughout this book; listed here are the book titles, authors and the page numbers on which to locate each book's description, publisher and current price as of 1990.

## I. Employment Opportunities

Animation Industry Directory,  24

## II. Learning to Draw

Drawing the Head and Figure (Jack Hamm),  29
Figure Drawing For All It's Worth (Andrew Loomis),  29
Drawing the Head and Hands (Andrew Loomis), 29
Anatomy (Joseph Sheppard),  30
Artistic Anatomy (Dr. Paul Richer and Robert Beverly Hale),  30
Drawing the Human Form (William A. Berry),  30
The Natural Way to Draw (Kimon Nicolaides),  30
The Human Figure—A Photographic Reference for Artists (Erik A. Ruby),  30
How to Draw Animals (Jack Hamm),  30
The Art of Animal Drawing (Ken Hultgren),  31

## III. Learning to Animate

Animation (Preston Blair),  40
How To Animate Film Cartoons (Preston Blair),  40, 48, 50
Disney Animation: The Illusion of Life (Frank Thomas and Ollie Johnston),  40
The Human Figure in Motion (Eadweard Muybridge),  45
Animals in Motion (Eadweard Muybridge),  45

## V. Writing for Animation

Screenplay (Syd Field),  71
Adventures in the Screen Trade (William Goldman),  71
On Becoming a Novelist (John Gardner),  71
The Art of Fiction (John Gardner),  71
The Art of Dramatic Writing (Lajos Egri),  72
The Art of Creative Writing (Lajos Egri),  72
Taking It All In (Pauline Kael),  72

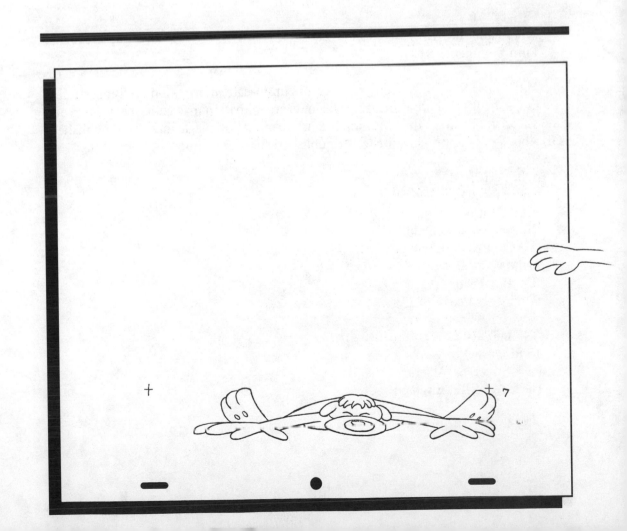

## VI. Directing Animation Films

Grammar of the Film Language (Daniel Arijon),  79
On Film Editing (Edward Dmytryk),  81
The Animation Book (Kit Laybourne),  83
The World of Animation (Kodak series),  83
The Complete Kodak Animation Book (Kodak series),  83

## VII. The Animation Film Producer

The Movie Brats (Michael Pye and Linda Myles),  97
The Film Industries (Michael F. Mayer),  98
Independent Feature Film Production (Gregory Goodell),  98
Reel Power (Mark Litwak),  99
Indecent Exposure (David McClintick),  100


The following film trade journals and film magazines are also described in this book, on the pages listed.

Variety,  70
American Film,  81
Film Comment,  81

MAGAZINES on animation provide more up-to-date information on films, studios, screenings, books and other magazines. However, animation magazines have come and gone surprisingly often; the following is a list of animation magazines being published as this book goes to press. Write to the publishers for current subscription rates.

ANIMATION MAGAZINE
Circulation Manager
6750 Centinela Ave., Suite 300
Culver City, CA 90230

ANIMATO
P.O. Box 1240
Cambridge, Mass. 02238

ANIMATOR
13 Ringway Road
Park Street, St. Albans
Herts AL2 2RE, England

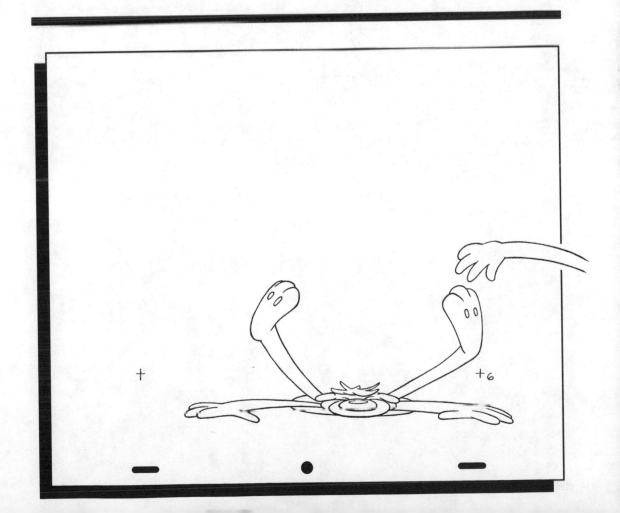

IN TOON
In Toon Publications
186 Engert Avenue
Brooklyn, N.Y. 11222

VIDEOCASSETTES of easy- and difficult-to-locate cartoon titles are available for sale through *The Whole Toon Catalog,* from Whole Toon Access, P.O. Box 369, 1460 19th Avenue N. W., Issaquah, Wash. 98027

The Laser Disc Newsletter is described on page 43; Suite 428, 496A Hudson Street, New York N.Y. 10014.

Private Snafu cartoons, the complete collection on videocassettes, as described on page 14, can be ordered from Bosko Video, 3802 E. Cudahy Avenue, Cudahy, WI 53110.

# INDEX

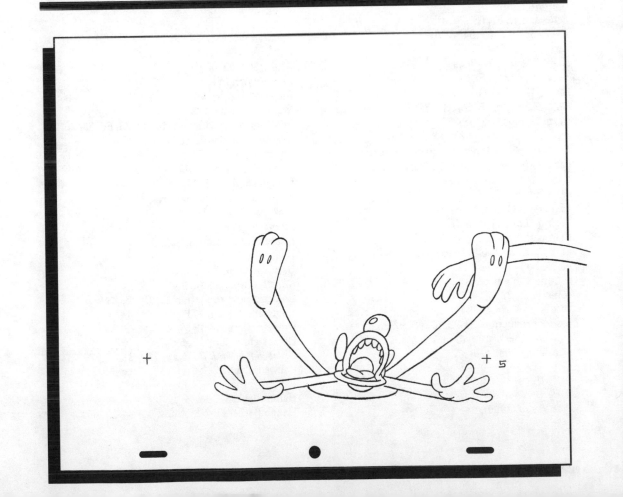

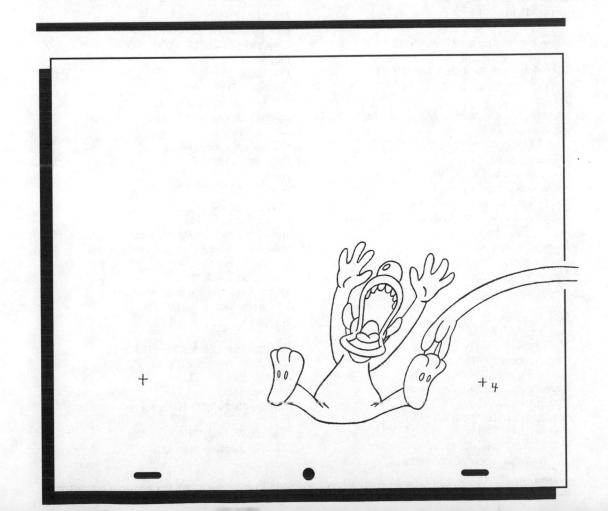

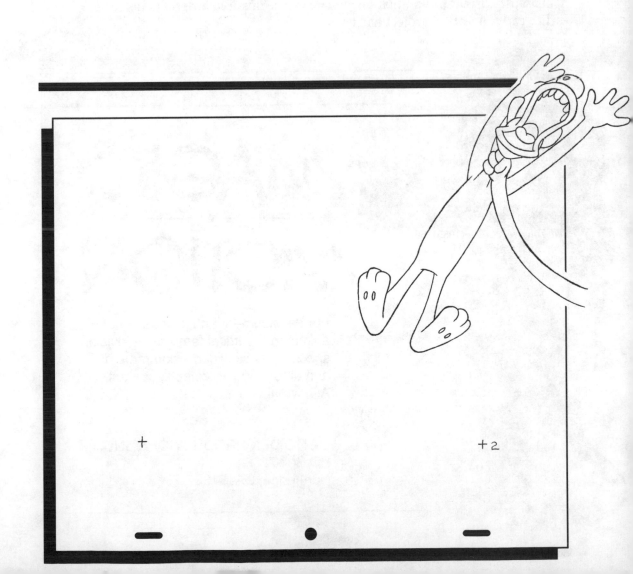

+

+2

# LION'S DEN PRODUCTIONS

LION'S DEN PRODUCTIONS successfully followed its own advice in chapter seven and raised independent financing to produce a feature length theatrical cartoon—a science fiction story about whales, told from the whales' point of view—and negotiations were well under way to secure a distribution deal with a major Hollywood film distributor. Part way into production the financial backers suffered a serious setback, so we quickly adapted our story and produced an excellent 24-minute cartoon (the proper length for a half-hour TV special) in Disney-style full animation. As this goes to press it is too early to know when this initial project will be revived as a full length theatrical feature, or when the completed shorter version will be aired on television.

Lion's Den has four other original stories for feature length theatrical cartoons in various stages of development, each one different from the other in subject and tone, and all of them fully adhering to the guidelines of intelligent writing outlined in chapters four and five. We are currently storyboarding one of these stories, which we hope in the current pro-animation climate will be financed for production as our earlier cartoon feature project had been.

© 1991 LDP

# MAGIC *in* MOTION

For development and production of animated theatrical features, television specials, music videos, commercials and other special projects, contact Al Lowenheim at:

LION'S DEN PRODUCTIONS, INC.
PO Box 7368
Northridge, CA  91327-7368